SCHOPENHAUER
AS EDUCATOR

by

Friedrich Nietzsche

translated by

Adrian Collins

I

1

WHEN the traveller, who had seen many countries and nations and continents, was asked what common attribute he had found everywhere existing among men, he answered, "They have a tendency to sloth." Many may think that the fuller truth would have been, "They are all timid." They hide themselves behind "manners" and "opinions." At bottom every man knows well enough that he is a unique being, only once on this earth; and by no extraordinary chance will such a marvellously picturesque piece of diversity in unity as he is, ever be put together a second time. He knows this, but hides it like an evil conscience;—and why? From fear of his neighbour, who looks for the latest conventionalities in him, and is wrapped up in them himself. But what is it that forces the man to fear his neighbour, to think and act with his herd, and not seek his own joy? Shyness perhaps, in a few rare cases, but in the majority it is idleness, the "taking things easily," in a word the "tendency to sloth," of which the traveller spoke. He was right; men are more slothful than timid, and their greatest fear is of the burdens that an uncompromising honesty and nakedness of speech and action would lay on them. It is only the artists who hate this lazy wandering in borrowed manners and ill-fitting opinions, and discover the secret of the evil conscience, the truth that each human being is a unique marvel. They show us, how in every little movement of his muscles the man is an individual self, and further—as an analytical deduction from his individuality—a beautiful and interesting object, a new and incredible phenomenon (as is every work of nature), that can never become tedious. If the great thinker despise mankind, it is for their laziness; they seem mere indifferent bits of pottery, not worth any commerce or improvement. The man who will not belong to the general mass, has only to stop "taking himself easily"; to follow his conscience, which cries out to him, "Be thyself! all that thou doest and thinkest and desirest, is not thyself!"

Every youthful soul hears this cry day and night, and quivers to hear it: for she divines the sum of happiness that has been from eternity destined for her, if she think of her true deliverance; and towards this happiness she can in no wise be helped, so long as she lies in the chains of Opinion and of Fear. And how comfortless and unmeaning may life become without this deliverance! There is no more desolate or Ishmaelitish creature in nature than the man who has broken away from his true genius, and does nothing but peer aimlessly about him. There is no reason to attack such a man at all, for he is a mere husk without a kernel, a painted cloth, tattered and sagging, a scarecrow ghost, that can rouse no fear, and certainly no pity. And though one be right in saying of a sluggard that he is "killing time" yet in respect of an age that rests its salvation on public opinion,—that is, on private laziness,—one must be quite determined that such a time shall be "killed," once and for all: I mean that it shall be blotted from life's true History of Liberty. Later generations will be greatly disgusted, when they come to treat the movements of a period in which no living men ruled, but shadow-men on the screen of public opinion; and to some far posterity our age may well be the darkest chapter of history, the most unknown because the least human. I have walked through the new streets of our cities, and thought how of all the dreadful houses that these gentlemen with their public opinion have built for themselves, not a stone will remain in a hundred years, and that the opinions of these busy masons may well have fallen with them. But how full of hope should they all be who feel that they are no citizens of this age! If they were, they would have to help on the work of "killing their time," and of perishing with it,—when they wish rather to quicken the time to life, and in that life themselves to *live*.

But even if the future leave us nothing to hope for, the wonderful fact of our existing at this present moment of time gives us the greatest encouragement to live after our own rule and measure; so inexplicable is it, that we should be living just to-day, though there have been an infinity of time wherein we might have arisen; that we own nothing but a span's length of it, this "to-day" and must show in it wherefore and whereunto we have arisen. We have to answer for our existence to ourselves; and will therefore be our own true pilots, and not admit that our being resembles a blind fortuity. One must take a rather impudent and reckless way with the riddle; especially as the key is apt to be lost, however things turn out. Why cling to your bit of earth, or your little business, or listen to what your neighbour says? It is so provincial to bind oneself to views which are no longer binding a couple of hundred miles away. East and West are signs that somebody chalks up in front of us to fool such cowards as we are. "I will make the attempt to gain freedom," says the youthful soul; and will be hindered, just because two nations happen to hate each other and go to war, or because there is a sea between two parts of the earth, or a religion is taught in the vicinity, which did not exist two thousand years ago. "And this is not—thyself," the soul says. "No one can build thee the bridge, over which thou must cross the river of life, save thyself alone. There are paths and bridges and demi-gods without number, that will gladly carry thee over, but only at the price of thine own self: thy self wouldst thou have to give in pawn, and then lose it. There is in the world one road whereon none may go, except thou: ask not whither it lead, but go forward. Who was it that spake that true word—'A man has never risen higher than when he knoweth not whither his road may yet lead him'?"

But how can we "find ourselves" again, and how can man "know himself"? He is a thing obscure and veiled: if the hare have seven skins, man can cast from him seventy times seven, and yet will not be able to say "Here art thou in very truth; this is outer shell no more." Also this digging into one's self, this straight, violent descent into the pit of one's being, is a troublesome and dangerous business to start. A man may easily take such hurt, that no physician can heal him. And again, what were the use, since everything bears witness to our essence,—our friendships and enmities, our looks and greetings, our memories and forgetfulnesses, our books and our writing! This is the most effective way: to let the youthful soul look back on life with the question, "What hast thou up to now truly loved, what has drawn thy soul upward, mastered it and blessed it too?" Set up these things that thou hast honoured before thee, and, maybe, they will show thee, in their being and their order, a law which is the fundamental law of thine own self. Compare these objects, consider how one completes and broadens and transcends and explains another, how they form a ladder on which thou hast all the time been climbing to thy self: for thy true being lies not deeply hidden in thee, but an infinite height above thee, or at least above that which thou dost commonly take to be thyself. The true educators and moulders reveal to thee the real groundwork and import of thy being, something that in itself cannot be moulded or educated, but is anyhow difficult of approach, bound and crippled: thy educators can be nothing but thy deliverers. And that is the secret of all culture: it does not give artificial limbs, wax noses, or spectacles for the eyes—a thing that could buy such gifts is but the base coin of education. But it is rather a liberation, a removal of all the weeds and rubbish and vermin that attack the delicate shoots, the streaming forth of light and warmth, the tender dropping of the night rain; it is the following and the adoring of Nature when she is pitifully-minded as a mother;—her completion, when it bends before her fierce and ruthless blasts and turns them to good, and draws a veil over all expression of her tragic unreason—for she is a step-mother too, sometimes.

There are other means of "finding ourselves," of coming to ourselves out of the confusion wherein we all wander as in a dreary cloud; but I know none better than to think on our educators. So I will to-day take as my theme the hard teacher Arthur Schopenhauer, and speak of others later.

2

In order to describe properly what an event my first look into Schopenhauer's writings was for me, I must dwell for a minute on an idea, that recurred more constantly in my youth, and touched me more nearly, than any other. I wandered then as I pleased in a world of wishes, and thought that destiny would relieve me of the dreadful and wearisome duty of educating myself: some philosopher would come at the right moment to do it for me,—some true philosopher, who could be obeyed without further question, as he would be trusted more than one's self. Then I said within me: "What would be the principles, on which he might teach thee? "And I pondered in my mind what he would say to the two maxims of education that hold the field in our time. The first demands that the teacher should find out at once the strong point in his pupil, and then direct all his skill and will, all the moisture and all the sunshine, to bring the fruit of that single virtue to maturity. The second requires him to raise to a higher power all the qualities that already exist, cherish them and bring them into a harmonious relation. But, we may ask, should one who has a decided talent for working in gold be made for that reason to learn music? And can we admit that Benvenuto Cellini's father was right in continually forcing him back to the "dear little horn"—the "cursed piping," as his son called it? We cannot think so in the case of such a strong and clearly marked talent as his, and it may well be that this maxim of harmonious development applies only to weaker natures, in which there is a whole swarm of desires and inclinations, though they may not amount to very much, singly or together. On the other hand, where do we find such a blending of harmonious voices—nay, the soul of harmony itself—as we see in natures like Cellini's, where everything—knowledge, desire, love and hate— tends towards a single point, the root of all, and a harmonious system, the resultant of the various forces, is built up through the irresistible domination of this vital centre? And so perhaps the two maxims are not contrary at all: the one merely saying that man must have a centre, the other, a circumference as well. The philosophic teacher of my dream would not only discover the central force, but would know how to prevent its being destructive of the other powers: his task, I thought, would be the welding of the whole man into a solar system with life and movement, and the discovery of its paraphysical laws.

In the meantime I could not find my philosopher, however I tried; I saw how badly we moderns compare with the Greeks and Romans, even in the serious study of educational problems. You can go through all Germany, and especially all the universities, with this need in your heart, and will not find what you seek; many humbler wishes than that are still unfulfilled there. For example, if a German seriously wish to make himself an orator, or to enter a "school for authors," he will find neither master nor school: no one yet seems to have thought that speaking and writing are arts which cannot be learnt without the most careful method and untiring application. But, to their shame, nothing shows more clearly the insolent self-satisfaction of our people than the lack of demand for educators; it comes partly from meanness, partly from want of thought. Anything will do as a so-called "family tutor," even among our most eminent and cultured people: and what a menagerie of crazy heads and mouldy devices mostly go to make up the belauded Gymnasium! And consider what we are satisfied with in our finishing schools,—our universities. Look at our professors and their institutions! And compare the difficulty of the task of educating a man to be a man! Above all, the wonderful way in which the German savants fall to their dish of knowledge, shows that they are thinking more of Science than mankind; and they are trained to lead a forlorn hope in her service, in order to encourage ever new generations to the same sacrifice. If their traffic with knowledge be not limited and controlled by any more general principles of education, but allowed to run on indefinitely,—"the more the better,"—it is as harmful to learning as the economic theory of *laisser faire* to common morality. No one recognises now that the education of the professors is an exceedingly difficult problem, if their humanity is not to be sacrificed or shrivelled up:—this difficulty can be actually seen in countless examples of natures warped and twisted by their reckless and premature devotion to science. There is a still more important testimony to the complete absence of higher education, pointing to a greater and more universal danger. It is clear at once why an orator or writer cannot now be educated,—because there are no teachers; and why a savant must be a distorted and perverted thing,—because he will have been trained by the inhuman abstraction, science. This being so, let a man ask himself: "Where are now the types of moral excellence and fame for all our generation—learned and unlearned, high and low— the visible abstract of constructive ethics for this age? Where has vanished all the reflection on moral questions that has occupied every great developed society at all epochs?" There is no fame for that now, and there are none to reflect: we are really drawing on the inherited moral capital which our predecessors accumulated for us, and which we do not know how to increase, but only to squander. Such things are either not mentioned in our society, or, if at all, with a naive want of personal experience that makes one disgusted. It comes to this, that our schools and professors simply turn aside from any moral instruction or content themselves with formulae; virtue is a word and nothing more, on both sides, an old-fashioned word that they laugh at—and it is worse when they do not laugh, for then they are hypocrites.

An explanation of this faint-heartedness and ebbing of all moral strength would be difficult and complex: but whoever is considering the influence of Christianity in its hour of victory on the morality of the mediaeval world, must not forget that it reacts also in its defeat, which is apparently its position to-day. By its lofty ideal, Christianity has outbidden the ancient Systems of Ethics and their invariable naturalism, with which men came to feel a dull disgust: and afterwards when they did reach the knowledge of what was better and higher, they found they had no longer the power, for all their desire, to return to its embodiment in the antique virtues. And so the life of the modern man is passed in see-sawing between Christianity and Paganism, between a furtive or hypocritical approach to Christian morality, and an equally shy and spiritless dallying with the antique: and he does not thrive under it. His inherited fear of naturalism, and its more recent attraction for him, his desire to come to rest somewhere, while in the impotence of his intellect he swings backwards and forwards between the "good" and the "better" course— all this argues an instability in the modern mind that condemns it to be without joy or fruit. Never were moral teachers more necessary and never were they more unlikely to be found: physicians are most in danger themselves in times when they are most needed and many men are sick. For where are our modern physicians who are strong and sure-footed enough to hold up another or lead him by the hand? There lies a certain heavy gloom on the best men of our time, an eternal loathing for the battle that is fought in their hearts between honesty and lies, a wavering of trust in themselves, which makes them quite incapable of showing to others the way they must go.

So I was right in speaking of my "wandering in a world of wishes" when I dreamt of finding a true philosopher who could lift me from the slough of insufficiency, and teach me again simply and honestly—to be in my thoughts and life, in the deepest sense of the word, "out of season"; simply and honestly for men have now become such complicated machines that they must be dishonest, if they speak at all, or wish to act on their words.

With such needs and desires within me did I come to know Schopenhauer.

I belong to those readers of Schopenhauer who know perfectly well, after they have turned the first page, that they will read all the others, and listen to every word that he has spoken. My trust in him sprang to life at once, and has been the same for nine years. I understood him as though he had written for me (this is the most intelligible, though a rather foolish and conceited way of expressing it). Hence I never found a paradox in him, though occasionally some small errors: for paradoxes are only assertions that carry no conviction, because the author has made them himself without any conviction, wishing to appear brilliant, or to mislead, or, above all, to pose. Schopenhauer never poses: he writes for himself, and no one likes to be deceived—least of all a philosopher who has set this up as his law: "deceive nobody, not even thyself," neither with the "white lies" of all social intercourse, which writers almost unconsciously imitate, still less with the more conscious deceits of the platform, and the artificial methods of rhetoric. Schopenhauer's speeches are to himself alone; or if you like to imagine an auditor, let it be a son whom the father is instructing. It is a rough, honest, good-humoured talk to one who "hears and loves." Such writers are rare. His strength and sanity surround us at the first sound of his voice: it is like entering the heights of the forest, where we breathe deep and are well again. We feel a bracing air everywhere, a certain candour and naturalness of his own, that belongs to men who are at home with themselves, and masters of a very rich home indeed: he is quite different from the writers who are surprised at themselves if they have said something intelligent, and whose pronouncements for that reason have something nervous and unnatural about them. We are just as little reminded in Schopenhauer of the professor with his stiff joints worse for want of exercise, his narrow chest and scraggy figure, his slinking or strutting gait. And again his rough and rather grim soul leads us not so much to miss as to despise the suppleness and courtly grace of the excellent Frenchmen; and no one will find in him the gilded imitations of pseudo-gallicism that our German writers prize so highly. His style in places reminds me a little of Goethe, but is not otherwise on any German model. For he knows how to be profound with simplicity, striking without rhetoric, and severely logical without pedantry: and of what German could he have learnt that? He also keeps free from the hair-splitting, jerky and (with all respect) rather un-German manner of Lessing: no small merit in him, for Lessing is the most tempting of all models for prose style. The highest praise I can give his manner of presentation is to apply his own phrase to himself:—"A philosopher must be very honest to avail himself of no aid from poetry or rhetoric." That honesty is something, and even a virtue, is one of those private opinions which are forbidden in this age of public opinion; and so I shall not be praising Schopenhauer, but only giving him a distinguishing mark, when I repeat that he is honest, even as a writer: so few of them are that we are apt to mistrust every one who writes at all. I only know a single author that I can rank with Schopenhauer, or even above him, in the matter of honesty; and that is Montaigne. The joy of living on this earth is increased by the existence of such a man. The effect on myself, at any rate, since my first acquaintance with that strong and masterful spirit, has been, that I can say of him as he of Plutarch—"As soon as I open him, I seem to grow a pair of wings." If I had the task of making myself at home on the earth, I would choose him as my companion.

Schopenhauer has a second characteristic in common with Montaigne, besides honesty; a joy that really makes others joyful. "*Aliis laetus, sibi sapiens.*" There are two very different kinds of joyfulness. The true thinker always communicates joy and life, whether he is showing his serious or comic side, his human insight or his godlike forbearance: without surly looks or trembling hands or watery eyes, but simply and truly, with fearlessness and strength, a little cavalierly perhaps, and sternly, but always as a conqueror: and it is this that brings the deepest and intensest joy, to see the conquering god with all the monsters that he has fought. But the joyfulness one finds here and there in the mediocre writers and limited thinkers makes some of us miserable; I felt this, for example, with the "joyfulness" of David Strauss. We are generally ashamed of such a quality in our contemporaries, because they show the nakedness of our time, and of the men in it, to posterity. Such *fils de joie* do not see the sufferings and the monsters, that they pretend, as philosophers, to see and fight; and so their joy deceives us, and we hate it; it tempts to the false belief that they have gained some victory. At bottom there is only joy where there is victory: and this applies to true philosophy as much as to any work of art. The contents may be forbidding and serious, as the problem of existence always is; the work will only prove tiresome and oppressive, if the slipshod thinker and the dilettante have spread the mist of their insufficiency over it: while nothing happier or better can come to man's lot than to be near one of those conquering spirits whose profound thought has made them love what is most vital, and whose wisdom has found its goal in beauty. They really speak: they are no stammerers or babblers; they live and move, and have no part in the *danse macabre* of the rest of humanity. And so in their company one feels a natural man again, and could cry out with Goethe—"What a wondrous and priceless thing is a living creature! How fitted to his surroundings, how true, and real!"

I have been describing nothing but the first, almost physiological, impression made upon me by Schopenhauer, the magical emanation of inner force from one plant of Nature to another, that follows the slightest contact. Analysing it, I find that this influence of Schopenhauer has three elements, his honesty, his joy, and his consistency. He is honest, as speaking and writing for himself alone; joyful, because his thought has conquered the greatest difficulties; consistent, because he cannot help being so. His strength rises like a flame in the calm air, straight up, without a tremor or deviation. He finds his way, without our noticing that he has been seeking it: so surely and cleverly and inevitably does he run his course, as if by some law of gravitation. If any one have felt what it means to find, in our present world of Centaurs and Chimaeras, a single-hearted and unaffected child of nature who moves unconstrained on his own road, he will understand my joy and surprise in discovering Schopenhauer: I knew in him the educator and philosopher I had so long desired. Only, however, in his writings: which was a great loss. All the more did I exert myself to see behind the book the living man whose testament it was, and who promised his inheritance to such as could, and would, be more than his readers—his pupils and his sons.

3

I get profit from a philosopher, just so far as he can be an example to me. There is no doubt that a man can draw whole nations after him by his example; as is shown by Indian history, which is practically the history of Indian philosophy. But this example must exist in his outward life, not merely in his books ; it must follow the way of the Grecian philosophers, whose doctrine was in their dress and bearing and general manner of life rather than in their speech or writing. We have nothing yet of this "breathing testimony" in German philosophical life; the spirit has, apparently, long completed its emancipation, while the flesh has hardly begun; yet it is foolish to think that the spirit can be really free and independent when this victory over limitation—which is ultimately a formative limiting of one's self—is not embodied anew in every look and movement. Kant held to his university, submitted to its regulations, and belonged, as his colleagues and students thought, to a definite religious faith: and naturally his example has produced, above all, University professors of philosophy. Schopenhauer makes small account of the learned tribe, keeps himself exclusive, and cultivates an independence from state and society as his ideal, to escape the chains of circumstance here : that is his value to us. Many steps in the enfranchisement of the philosopher are unknown in Germany; they cannot always remain so. Our artists live more bravely and honourably than our philosophers; and Richard Wagner, the best example of all, shows how genius need not fear a fight to the death with the established forms and ordinances, if we wish to bring the higher truth and order, that lives in him, to the light. The "truth," however, of which we hear so much from our professors, seems to be a far more modest being, and no kind of disturbance is to be feared from her; she is an easy-going and pleasant creature, who is continually assuring the powers that be that no one need fear any trouble from her quarter: for man is only "pure reason." And therefore I will say, that philosophy in Germany has more and more to learn not to be "pure reason": and it may well take as its model "Schopenhauer the man."

It is no less than a marvel that he should have come to be this human kind of example: for he was beset, within and without, by the most frightful dangers, that would have crushed and broken a weaker nature. I think there was a strong likelihood of Schopenhauer the man going under, and leaving at best a residue of "pure reason": and only "at best"—it was more probable that neither man nor reason would survive.

A modern Englishman sketches the most usual danger to extraordinary men who live in a society that worships the ordinary, in this manner:—"Such uncommon characters are first cowed, then become sick and melancholy, and then die. A Shelley could never have lived in England: a race of Shelleys would have been impossible." Our Hölderlins and Kleists were undone by their unconventionality, and were not strong enough for the climate of the so-called German culture; and only iron natures like Beethoven, Goethe, Schopenhauer and Wagner could hold out against it. Even in them the effect of this weary toiling and moiling is seen in many lines and wrinkles; their breathing is harder and their voice is forced. The old diplomatist who had only just seen and spoken to Goethe, said to a friend—"Voilà un homme qui a eu de grands chagrins!" which Goethe translated to mean "That is a man who has taken great pains in his life." And he adds, "If the trace of the sorrow and activity we have gone through cannot be wiped from our features, it is no wonder that all that survives of us and our struggles should bear the same impress." And this is the Goethe to whom our cultured Philistines point as the happiest of Germans, that they may prove their thesis, that it must be possible to be happy among them—with the unexpressed corollary that no one can be pardoned for feeling unhappy and lonely among them. Hence they push their doctrine, in practice, to its merciless conclusion, that there is always a secret guilt in isolation. Poor Schopenhauer had this secret guilt too in his heart, the guilt of cherishing his philosophy more than his fellow-men; and he was so unhappy as to have learnt from Goethe that he must defend his philosophy at all costs from the neglect of his contemporaries, to save its very existence: for there is a kind of Grand Inquisitor's Censure in which the Germans, according to Goethe, are great adepts: it is called—inviolable silence. This much at least was accomplished by it; the greater part of the first edition of Schopenhauer's masterpiece had to be turned into waste paper. The imminent risk that his great work would be undone, merely by neglect, bred in him a state of unrest—perilous and uncontrollable;—for no single adherent of any note presented himself. It is tragic to watch his search for any evidence of recognition: and his piercing cry of triumph at last, that he would now really be read (*legor et legar*), touches us with a thrill of pain. All the traits in which we do not see the great philosopher show us the suffering man, anxious for his noblest possessions; he was tortured by the fear of losing his little property, and perhaps of no longer being able to maintain in its purity his truly antique attitude towards philosophy. He often chose falsely in his desire to find real trust and compassion in men, only to return with a heavy heart to his faithful dog again. He was absolutely alone, with no single friend of his own kind to comfort him; and between one and none there lies an infinity—as ever between something and nothing. No one who has true friends knows what real loneliness means, though he may have the whole world in antagonism round him. Ah, I see well ye do not know what isolation is! Whenever there are great societies with governments and religions and public opinions where there is a tyranny, in short, there will the lonely philosopher be hated: for philosophy offers an asylum to mankind where no tyranny can penetrate, the inner sanctuary, the centre of the heart's labyrinth: and the tyrants are galled at it. Here do the lonely men lie hid: but here too lurks their greatest danger. These men who have saved their inner freedom, must also live and be seen in the outer world: they stand in countless human relations by their birth, position, education and country, their own circumstances and the importunity of others: and so they are presumed to hold an immense number of opinions, simply because these happen to prevail: every look that is not a denial counts as an assent, every motion of the hand that does not destroy is regarded as an aid. These free and lonely men know that they perpetually seem other than they are. While they wish for nothing but truth and honesty, they are in a net of misunderstanding; and that ardent desire cannot prevent a mist of false opinions, of adaptations and wrong conclusions, of partial misapprehension and intentional reticence, from gathering round their actions, And there settles a cloud of melancholy on their brows : for such natures hate the necessity of pretence worse than death : and the continual bitterness gives them a threatening and volcanic character. They take revenge from time to time for their forced concealment and self-restraint: they issue from their dens with lowering looks: their words and deeds are explosive, and may lead to their own destruction. Schopenhauer lived amid dangers of this sort. Such lonely men need love, and friends, to whom they can be as open and sincere as to themselves, and in whose presence the deadening silence and hypocrisy may cease. Take their friends away, and there is left an increasing peril; Heinrich von Kleist was broken by the lack of love, and the most terrible weapon against unusual men is to drive them into themselves; and then their issuing forth again is a volcanic eruption. Yet there are always some demi-gods who can bear life under these fearful conditions and can be their conquerors: and if you would hear their lonely chant, listen to the music of Beethoven.

So the first danger in whose shadow Schopenhauer lived was—isolation. The second is called—doubting of the truth. To this every thinker is liable who sets out from the philosophy of Kant, provided he be strong and sincere in his sorrows and his desires, and not a mere tinkling thought-box or calculating machine. We all know the shameful state of things implied by this last reservation, and I believe it is only a very few men that Kant has so vitally affected as to change the current of their blood. To judge from what one reads, there must have been a revolution in every domain of thought since the work of this unobtrusive professor: I cannot believe it myself. For I see men, though darkly, as themselves needing to be revolutionised, before any "domains of thought" can be so. In fact, we find the first mark of any influence Kant may have had on the popular mind, in a corrosive scepticism and relativity. But it is only in noble and active spirits who could never rest in doubt that the shattering despair of truth itself could take the place of doubt. This was, for example, the effect of the Kantian philosophy on Heinrich von Kleist. "It was only a short time ago," he writes in his poignant way, "that I became acquainted with the Kantian philosophy; and I will tell you my thought, though I cannot fear that it will rack you to your inmost soul, as it did me.—We cannot decide, whether what we call truth is really truth, or whether it only seems so to us. If the latter, the truth that we amass here does not exist after death, and all our struggle to gain a possession that may follow us even to the grave is in vain. If the blade of this thought do not cut your heart, yet laugh not at another who feels himself wounded by it in his Holy of Holies. My one highest aim has vanished, and I have no more." Yes, when will men feel again deeply as Kleist did, and learn to measure a philosophy by what it means to the "Holy of Holies"? And yet we must make this estimate of what Schopenhauer can mean to us, after Kant, as the first pioneer to bring us from the heights of sceptical disillusionment or "critical" renunciation, to the greater height of tragic contemplation, the nocturnal heaven with its endless crown of stars. His greatness is that he can stand opposite the picture of life, and interpret it to us as a whole: while all the clever people cannot escape the error of thinking one comes nearer to the interpretation by a laborious analysis of the colours and material of the picture ; with the confession, probably, that the texture of the canvas is very complicated, and the chemical composition of the colours undiscoverable. Schopenhauer knew that one must guess the painter in order to understand the picture. But now the whole learned fraternity is engaged on understanding the colours and canvas, and not the picture: and only he who has kept the universal panorama of life and being firmly before his eyes, will use the individual sciences without harm to himself; for, without this general view as a norm, they are threads that lead nowhere and only confuse still more the maze of our existence. Here we see, as I said, the greatness of Schopenhauer, that he follows up every idea, as Hamlet follows the Ghost, without allowing himself to turn aside for a learned digression, or be drawn away by the scholastic abstractions of a rabid dialectic. The study of the minute philosophers is only interesting for the recognition that they have reached those stages in the great edifice of philosophy where learned disquisitions for and against, where hair-splitting objections and counter-objections are the rule: and for that reason they evade the demand of every great philosophy to speak *sub specie aeternitatis*—"this is the picture of the whole of life: learn thence the meaning of thine own life." And the converse: "read thine own life, and understand thence the hieroglyphs of the universal life." In this way must Schopenhauer's philosophy always be interpreted ; as an individualist philosophy, starting from the single man, in his own nature, to gain an insight into his personal miseries, and needs, and limitations, and find out the remedies that will console them: namely, the sacrifice of the ego, and its submission to the nobler ends, especially those of justice and mercy. He teaches us to distinguish between the true and the apparent furtherance of man's happiness: how neither the attainment of riches, nor honour, nor learning, can raise the individual from his deep despair at his unworthiness; and how the quest for these good things can only have meaning through a universal end that transcends and explains them;—the gaining of power to aid our physical nature by them and, as far as may be, correct its folly and awkwardness. For one's self only, in the first instance: and finally, through one's self, for all. It is a task that leads to scepticism: for there is so much to be made better yet, in one and all!

Applying this to Schopenhauer himself, we come to the third and most intimate danger in which he lived, and which lay deep in the marrow of his being. Every one is apt to discover a limitation in himself, in his gifts of intellect as well as his moral will, that fills him with yearning and melancholy; and as he strives after holiness through a consciousness of sin, so, as an intellectual being, he has a deep longing after the "genius" in himself. This is the root of all true culture; and if we say this means the aspiration of man to be "born again" as saint and genius, I know that one need not be a Buddhist to understand the myth. We feel a strong loathing when we find talent without such aspiration, in the circle of the learned, or among the so-called educated; for we see that such men, with all their cleverness, are no aid but a hindrance to the beginnings of culture and the blossoming of genius, the aim of all culture. There is a rigidity in them, parallel to the cold arrogance of conventional virtue, which also remains at the opposite pole to true holiness. Schopenhauer's nature contained an extraordinarily dangerous dualism. Few thinkers have felt as he did the complete and unmistakable certainty of genius within them; and his genius made him the highest of all promises,—that there could be no deeper furrow than that which he was ploughing in the ground of the modern world. He knew one half of his being to be fulfilled according to its strength, with no other need; and he followed with greatness and dignity his vocation of consolidating his victory. In the other half there was a gnawing aspiration, which we can understand, when we hear that he turned away with a sad look from the picture of Rancé, the founder of the Trappists, with the words: "That is a matter of grace." For genius evermore yearns after holiness as it sees further and more clearly from its watch-tower than other men, deep into the reconciliation of Thought and Being, the kingdom of peace and the denial of the will, and up to that other shore, of which the Indians speak. The wonder is, that Schopenhauer's nature should have been so inconceivably stable and unshakable that it could neither be destroyed nor petrified by this yearning. Every one will understand this after the measure of his own character and greatness: none of us will understand it in the fulness of its meaning.

The more one considers these three dangers, the more extraordinary will appear his vigour in opposing them and his safety after the battle. True, he gained many scars and open wounds: and a cast of mind that may seem somewhat too bitter and pugnacious. But his single ideal transcends the highest humanity in him. Schopenhauer stands as a pattern to men, in spite of all those scars and scratches. We may even say, that what was imperfect and "all too human" in him, brings us nearer to him as a man, for we see a sufferer and a kinsman to suffering, not merely a dweller on the unattainable heights of genius.

These three constitutional dangers that threatened Schopenhauer, threaten us all. Each one of us bears a creative solitude within himself, and his consciousness of it forms an exotic aura of strangeness round him. Most men cannot endure it, because they are slothful, as I said, and because their solitude hangs round them a chain of troubles and burdens. No doubt, for the man with this heavy chain, life loses almost everything that one desires from it in youth—joy, safety, honour: his fellow-men pay him his due of—isolation! The wilderness and the cave are about him, wherever he may live. He must look to it that he be not enslaved and oppressed, and become melancholy thereby. And let him surround himself with the pictures of good and brave fighters such as Schopenhauer.

The second danger, too, is not rare. Here and there we find one dowered by nature with a keen vision ; his thoughts dance gladly in the witches' Sabbath of dialectic; and if he uncautiously give his talent the rein, it is easy to lose all humanity and live a ghostly life in the realm of "pure reason": or through the constant search for the "pros and cons" of things, he may go astray from the truth and live without courage or confidence, in doubt, denial and discontent, and the slender hope that waits on disillusion: "No dog could live long thus!"

The third danger is a moral or intellectual hardening: man breaks the bond that united him to his ideal: he ceases to be fruitful and reproduce himself in this or that province, and becomes an enemy or a parasite of culture. The solitude of his being has become an indivisible, unrelated atom, an icy stone. And one can perish of this solitude as well as of the fear of it, of one's self as well as one's self-sacrifice, of both aspiration and petrifaction: and to live is ever to be in danger.

Beside these dangers to which Schopenhauer would have been constitutionally liable, in whatever century he had lived, there were also some produced by his own time; and it is essential to distinguish between these two kinds, in order to grasp the typical and formative elements in his nature. The philosopher casts his eye over existence, and wishes to give it a new standard value; for it has been the peculiar task of all great thinkers to be law-givers for the weight and stamp in the mint of reality. And his task will be hindered if the men he sees near him be a weakly and worm-eaten growth. To be correct in his calculation of existence, the unworthiness of the present time must be a very small item in the addition. The study of ancient or foreign history is valuable, if at all, for a correct judgment on the whole destiny of man; which must be drawn not only from an average estimate but from a comparison of the highest destinies that can befall individuals or nations. The present is too much with us; it directs the vision even against the philosopher's will: and it will inevitably be reckoned too high in the final sum. And so he must put a low figure on his own time as against others, and suppress the present in his picture of life, as well as in himself; must put it into the background or paint it over; a difficult, and almost impossible task. The judgment of the ancient Greek philosophers on the value of existence means so much more than our own, because they had the full bloom of life itself before them, and their vision was untroubled by any felt dualism between their wish for freedom and beauty on the grand scale, and their search after truth, with its single question "What is the real *worth* of life? "Empedocles lived when Greek culture was full to overflowing with the joy of life, and all ages may take profit from his words; especially as no other great philosopher of that great time ventured to contradict them. Empedocles is only the clearest voice among them—they all say the same thing, if a man will but open his ears. A modern thinker is always in the throes of an unfulfilled desire; he is looking for life,—warm, red life,—that he may pass judgment on it: at any rate he will think it necessary to be a living man himself, before he can believe in his power of judging. And this is the title of the modern philosophers to sit among the great aiders of Life (or rather of the will to live), and the reason why they can look from their own out-wearied time and aspire to a truer culture, and a clearer explanation. Their yearning is, however, their danger; the reformer in them struggles with the critical philosopher. And whichever way the victory incline, it also implies a defeat. How was Schopenhauer to escape this danger ?

We like to consider the great man as the noble child of his age, who feels its defects more strongly and intimately than the smaller men: and therefore the struggle of the great man *against* his age is apparently nothing but a mad fight to the death with himself. Only apparently, however: he only fights the elements in his time that hinder his own greatness, in other words his own freedom and sincerity. And so, at bottom, he is only an enemy to that element which is not truly himself, the irreconcilable antagonism of the temporal and eternal in him. The supposed "child of his age" proves to be but a step-child. From boyhood Schopenhauer strove with his time, a false and unworthy mother to him, and as soon as he had banished her, he could bring back his being to its native health and purity. For this very reason we can use his writings as mirrors of his time; it is no fault of the mirror if everything contemporary appear in it stricken by a ravaging disease, pale and thin, with tired looks and hollow eyes,—the step-child's sorrow made visible. The yearning for natural strength, for a healthy and simple humanity, was a yearning for himself: and as soon as he had conquered his time within him, he was face to face with his own genius. The secret of nature's being and his own lay open, the step-mother's plot to conceal his genius from him was foiled. And now he could turn a fearless eye towards the question, "What is the real worth of life?" without having any more to weigh a bloodless and chaotic age of doubt and hypocrisy. He knew that there was something higher and purer to be won on this earth than the life of his time, and a man does bitter wrong to existence who only knows it and criticises it in this hateful form. Genius, itself the highest product of life, is now summoned to justify life, if it can: the noble creative soul must answer the question:—"Dost thou in thy heart say 'Yea!' unto this existence? Is it enough for thee? Wilt thou be its advocate and its redeemer? One true 'Yea' from thy lips, and the sorely accused life shall go free." How shall he answer? In the words of Empedocles.

4

The last hint may well remain obscure for a time: I have something more easy to explain, namely how Schopenhauer can help us to educate ourselves *in opposition to* our age, since we have the advantage of really knowing our age, through him;—if it be an advantage! It may be no longer possible in a couple, of hundred years. I sometimes amuse myself with the idea that men may soon grow tired of books and their authors, and the savant of to-morrow come to leave directions in his will that his body be burned in the midst of his books, including of course his own writings. And in the gradual clearing of the forests, might not our libraries be very reasonably used for straw and brushwood? Most books are born from the smoke and vapour of the brain: and to vapour and smoke may they well return. For having no fire within themselves, they shall be visited with fire. And possibly to a later century our own may count as the "Dark age," because our productions heated the furnace hotter and more continuously than ever before. We are anyhow happy that we can learn to know our time; and if there be any sense in busying ourselves with our time at all, we may as well do it as thoroughly as we can, so that no one may have any doubt about it. The possibility of this we owe to Schopenhauer.

Our happiness would of course be infinitely greater, if our inquiry showed that nothing so hopeful and splendid as our present epoch had ever existed. There are simple people in some corner of the earth to-day—perhaps in Germany—who are disposed to believe in all seriousness that the world was put right two years ago, and that all stern and gloomy views of life are now contradicted by "facts." The foundation of the New German Empire is, to them, the decisive blow that annihilates all the "pessimistic" philosophers,—no doubt of it. To judge the philosopher's significance in our time, as an educator, we must oppose a widespread view like this, especially common in our universities. We must say, it is a shameful thing that such abominable flattery of the Time-Fetish should be uttered by a herd of so-called reflective and honourable men; it is a proof that we no longer see how far the seriousness of philosophy is removed from that of a newspaper. Such men have lost the last remnant of feeling, not only for philosophy, but also for religion, and have put in its place a spirit not so much of optimism as of journalism, the evil spirit that broods over the day—and the daily paper. Every philosophy that believes the problem of existence to be shelved, or even solved, by a political event, is a sham philosophy. There have been innumerable states founded since the beginning of the world; that is an old story. How should a political innovation manage once and for all to make a contented race of the dwellers on this earth? If any one believe in his heart that this is possible, he should report himself to our authorities : he really deserves to be Professor of Philosophy in a German university, like Harms in Berlin, Jürgen Meyer in Bonn, and Carriere in Munich.

We are feeling the consequences of the doctrine, preached lately from all the housetops, that the state is the highest end of man and there is no higher duty than to serve it: I regard this not a relapse into paganism, but into stupidity. A man who thinks state-service to be his highest duty, very possibly knows no higher one; yet there are both men and duties in a region beyond,—and one of these duties, that seems to me at least of higher value than state-service, is to destroy stupidity in all its forms—and this particular stupidity among them. And I have to do with a class of men whose teleological conceptions extend further than the well-being of a state, I mean with philosophers—and only with them in their relation to the world of culture, which is again almost independent of the "good of the state." Of the many links that make up the twisted chain of humanity, some are of gold and others of pewter.

How does the philosopher of our time regard culture? Quite differently, I assure you, from the professors who are so content with their new state. He seems to see the symptoms of an absolute uprooting of culture in the increasing rush and hurry of life, and the decay of all reflection and simplicity. The waters of religion are ebbing, and leaving swamps or stagnant pools : the nations are drawing away in enmity again, and long to tear each other in pieces. The sciences, blindly driving along, on a *laisser faire* system, without a common standard, are splitting up, and losing hold of every firm principle. The educated classes are being swept along in the contemptible struggle for wealth. Never was the world more worldly, never poorer in goodness and love. Men of learning are no longer beacons or sanctuaries in the midst of this turmoil of worldliness; they themselves are daily becoming more restless, thoughtless, loveless. Everything bows before the coming barbarism, art and science included. The educated men have degenerated into the greatest foes of education, for they will deny the universal sickness and hinder the physician. They become peevish, these poor nerveless creatures, if one speak of their weakness and combat the shameful spirit of lies in them. They would gladly make one believe that they have outstripped all the centuries, and they walk with a pretence of happiness which has something pathetic about it, because their happiness is so inconceivable. One would not even ask them, as Tannhäuser did Biterolf, "What hast thou, poor wretch, enjoyed!" For, alas! we know far better ourselves, in another way. There is a wintry sky over us, and we dwell on a high mountain, in danger and in need. Short-lived is all our joy, and the sun's rays strike palely on our white mountains. Music is heard; an old man grinds an organ, and the dancers whirl round, and the heart of the wanderer is shaken within him to see it: everything is so disordered, so drab, so hopeless. Even now there is a sound of joy, of clear thoughtless joy! but soon the mist of evening closes round, the note dies away, and the wanderer's footsteps are heard on the gravel; as far as his eye can reach there is nothing but the grim and desolate face of nature.

It may be one-sided, to insist only on the blurred lines and the dull colours in the picture of modern life: yet the other side is no more encouraging, it is only more disturbing. There is certainly strength there, enormous strength; but it is wild, primitive and merciless. One looks on with a chill expectancy, as though into the caldron of a witch's kitchen; every moment there may arise sparks and vapour, to herald some fearful apparition. For a century we have been ready for a world-shaking convulsion; and though we have lately been trying to set the conservative strength of the so-called national state against the great modern tendency to volcanic destructiveness, it will only be, for a long time yet, an aggravation of the universal unrest that hangs over us. We need not be deceived by individuals behaving as if they knew nothing of all this anxiety: their own restlessness shows how well they know it. They think more exclusively of themselves than men ever thought before; they plant and build for their little day, and the chase for happiness is never greater than when the quarry must be caught to-day or to-morrow: the next day perhaps there is no more hunting. We live in the Atomic Age, or rather in the Atomic Chaos. The opposing forces were practically held together in mediaeval times by the Church, and in some measure assimilated by the strong pressure which she exerted. When the common tie broke and the pressure relaxed, they rose once more against each other. The Reformation taught that many things were "adiaphora"—

departments that needed no guidance from religion: this was the price paid for its own existence. Christianity paid a similar one to guard itself against the far more religious antiquity: and laid the seeds of discord at once. Everything nowadays is directed by the fools and the knaves, the selfishness of the money-makers and the brute forces of militarism. The state in their hands makes a good show of reorganising everything, and of becoming the bond that unites the warring elements; in other words, it wishes for the same idolatry from mankind as they showed to the Church.

And we shall yet feel the consequences. We are even now on the ice-floes in the stream of the Middle Ages : they are thawing fast, and their movement is ominous : the banks are flooded, and giving way. The revolution, the atomistic revolution, is inevitable: but what *are* those smallest indivisible elements of human society?

There is surely far more danger to mankind in transitional periods like these than in the actual time of revolution and chaos; they are tortured by waiting, and snatch greedily at every moment; and this breeds all kinds of cowardice and selfishness in them: whereas the true feeling of a great and universal need ever inspires men, and makes them better. In the midst of such dangers, who will provide the guardians and champions for *Humanity*, for the holy and inviolate treasure that has been laid up in the temples, little by little, by countless generations? Who will set up again the *Image of Man*, when men in their selfishness and terror see nothing but the trail of the serpent or the cur in them, and have fallen from their high estate to that of the brute or the automaton?

There are three Images of Man fashioned by our modern time, which for a long while yet will urge mortal men to transfigure their own lives; they are the men of Rousseau, Goethe, and Schopenhauer. The first has the greatest fire, and is most calculated to impress the people: the second is only for the few, for those contemplative natures "in the grand style" who are misunderstood by the crowd. The third demands the highest activity in those who will follow it: only such men will look on that image without harm, for it breaks the spirit of that merely contemplative man, and the rabble shudder at it. From the first has come forth a strength that led and still leads to fearful revolution: for in all socialistic upheavals it is ever Rousseau's man who is the Typhoeus under the Etna. Oppressed and half crushed to death by the pride of caste and the pitilessness of wealth, spoilt by priests and bad education, a laughing-stock even to himself, man cries in his need on "holy mother Nature," and feels suddenly that she is as far from him as any god of the Epicureans. His prayers do not reach her; so deeply sunk is he in the Chaos of the unnatural. He contemptuously throws aside all the finery that seemed his truest humanity a little while ago—all his arts and sciences, all the refinements of his life,—he beats with his fists against the walls, in whose shadow he has degenerated, and goes forth to seek the light and the sun, the forest and the crag. And crying out, "Nature alone is good, the natural man alone is human," he despises himself and aspires beyond himself: a state wherein the soul is ready for a fearful resolve, but calls the noble and the rare as well from their utter depths.

Goethe's man is no such threatening force; in a certain sense he is a corrective and a sedative to those dangerous agitations of which Rousseau's man is a prey. Goethe himself in his youth followed the "gospel of kindly Nature" with all the ardour of his soul: his Faust was the highest and boldest picture of Rousseau's man, so far at any rate as his hunger for life, his discontent and yearning, his intercourse with the demons of the heart could be represented. But what comes from these congregated storm-clouds? Not a single lightning flash! And here begins the new Image of man the man according to Goethe. One might have thought that Faust would have lived a continual life of suffering, as a revolutionary and a deliverer, as the negative force that proceeds from goodness, as the genius of ruin, alike religious and daemonic, in opposition to his utterly un-daemonic companion ; though of course he could not be free of this companion, and had at once to use and despise his evil and destructive scepticism—which is the tragic destiny of all revolutionary deliverers. One is wrong, however, to expect anything of the sort: Goethe's man here parts company with Rousseau's; for he hates all violence, all sudden transition that is, all action: and the universal deliverer becomes merely the universal traveller. All the riches of life and nature, all antiquity—arts, mythologies and sciences—pass before his eager eyes, his deepest desires are aroused and satisfied, Helen herself can hold him no more and the moment must come for which his mocking companion is waiting. At a fair spot on the earth, his flight comes to an end: his pinions drop, and Mephistopheles is at his side. When the German ceases to be Faust, there is no danger greater than of becoming a Philistine and falling into the hands of the devil—heavenly powers alone can save him. Goethe's man is, as I said, the contemplative man in the grand style, who is only kept from dying of ennui by feeding on all the great and memorable things that have ever existed, and by living from desire to desire. He is not the active man; and when he does take a place among active men, as things are, you may be sure that no good will come of it (think, for example, of the zeal with which Goethe wrote for the stage!); and further, you may be sure that "things as they are" will suffer no change. Goethe's man is a conciliatory and conservative spirit, though in danger of degenerating into a Philistine, just as Rousseau's man may easily become a Catiline. All his virtues would be the better by the addition of a little brute force and elemental passion. Goethe appears to have seen where the weakness and danger of his creation lay, as is clear from Jarno's word to Wilhelm Meister: "You are bitter and ill-tempered—which is quite an excellent thing: if you could once become really angry, it would be still better." To speak plainly, it is necessary to become really angry in order that things may be better. The picture of Schopenhauer's man can help us here. *Schopenhauer's man voluntarily takes upon himself the pain of telling the truth*: this pain serves to quench his individual will and make him ready for the complete transformation of his being, which it is the inner meaning of life to realise. This openness in him appears to other men to be an effect of malice, for they think the preservation of their shifts and pretences to be the first duty of humanity, and any one who destroys their playthings to be merely malicious. They are tempted to cry out to such a man, in Faust's words to Mephistopheles:—

"So to the active and eternal
Creative force, in cold disdain
You now oppose the fist infernal"—

and he who would live according to Schopenhauer would seem to be more like a Mephistopheles than a Faust—that is, to our weak modern eyes, which always discover signs of malice in any negation. But there is a kind of denial and destruction that is the effect of that strong aspiration after holiness and deliverance, which Schopenhauer was the first philosopher to teach our profane and worldly generation. Everything that can be denied, deserves to be denied; and real sincerity means the belief in a state of things which cannot be denied, or in which there is no lie. The sincere man feels that his activity has a metaphysical meaning. It can only be explained by the laws of a different and a higher life; it is in the deepest sense an affirmation: even if everything that he does seem utterly opposed to the laws of our present life. It must lead therefore to constant suffering; but he knows, as Meister Eckhard did, that "the quickest beast that will carry you to perfection is suffering." Every one, I should think, who has such an ideal before him, must feel a wider sympathy; and he will have a burning desire to become a "Schopenhauer man";—pure and wonderfully patient, on his intellectual side full of a devouring fire, and far removed from the cold and contemptuous "neutrality" of the so-called scientific man; so high above any warped and morose outlook on life as to offer himself as the first victim of the truth he has won, with a deep consciousness of the sufferings that must spring from his sincerity. His courage will destroy his happiness on earth, he must be an enemy to the men he loves and the institutions in which he grew up, he must spare neither person nor thing, however it may hurt him, he will be misunderstood and thought an ally of forces that he abhors, in his search for righteousness he will seem unrighteous by human standards: but he must comfort himself with the words that his teacher Schopenhauer once used: "A happy life is impossible, the highest thing that man can aspire to is a *heroic* life; such as a man lives, who is always fighting against unequal odds for the good of others; and wins in the end without any thanks. After the battle is over, he stands like the Prince in the *re corvo* of Gozzi, with dignity and nobility in his eyes, but turned to stone. His memory remains, and will be reverenced as a hero's; his will, that has been mortified all his life by toiling and struggling, by evil payment and ingratitude, is absorbed into Nirvana." Such a heroic life, with its full "mortification"—corresponds very little to the paltry ideas of the people who talk most about it, and make festivals in memory of great men, in the belief that a great man is great in the sense that they are small, either through exercise of his gifts to please himself or by a blind mechanical obedience to this inner force ; so that the man who does not possess the gift or feel the compulsion has the same right to be small as the other to be great. But "gift" and "compulsion" are contemptible words, mere means of escape from an inner voice, a slander on him who has listened to the voice—the great man; he least of all will allow himself to be given or compelled to anything: for he knows as well as any smaller man how easily life can be taken and how soft the bed whereon he might lie if he went the pleasant and conventional way with himself and his fellow-creatures: all the regulations of mankind are turned to the end that the intense feeling of life may be lost in continual distractions. Now why will he so strongly choose the opposite, and try to feel life, which is the same as to suffer from life? Because he sees that men will tempt him to betray himself, and that there is a kind of agreement to draw him from his den. He will prick up his ears and gather himself together, and say, "I will remain mine own." He gradually comes to understand what a fearful decision it is. For he must go down into the depths of being, with a string of curious questions on his lips—"Why am I alive? what lesson have I to learn from life? how have I become what I am, and why do I suffer in this existence?" He is troubled, and sees that no one is troubled in the same way; but rather that the hands of his fellow-men are passionately stretched out towards the fantastic drama of the political theatre, or they themselves are treading the boards under many disguises, youths, men and graybeards, fathers, citizens, priests, merchants and officials,—busy with the comedy they are all playing, and never thinking of their own selves. To the question "To what end dost thou live?" they would all immediately answer, with pride, "To *become* a good citizen or professor or statesman,"—and yet they *are* something which can never be changed: and why are they just—this? Ah, and why nothing better? The man who only regards his life as a moment in the evolution of a race or a state or a science, and will belong merely to a history of "becoming," has not understood the lesson of existence, and must learn it over again. This eternal "becoming something" is a lying puppet-show, in which man has forgot himself; it is the force that scatters individuality to the four winds, the eternal childish game that the big baby time is playing in front of us—and with us. The heroism of sincerity lies in ceasing to be the plaything of time. Everything in the process of "becoming" is a hollow sham, contemptible and shallow: man can only find the solution of his riddle in "being" something definite and unchangeable. He begins to test how deep both "becoming" and "being" are rooted in him—and a fearful task is before his soul; to destroy the first, and bring all the falsity of things to the light. He wishes to know everything, not to feed a delicate taste, like Goethe's man, to take delight, from a safe place, in the multiplicity of existence: but he himself is the first sacrifice that he brings. The heroic man does not think of his happiness or misery, his virtues or his vices, or of his being the measure of things; he has no further hopes of himself and will accept the utter consequences of his hopelessness. His strength lies in his self-forgetfulness: if he have a thought for himself, it is only to measure the vast distance between himself and his aim, and to view what he has left behind him as so much dross. The old philosophers sought for happiness and truth, with all their strength: and there is an evil principle in nature that not one shall find that which he cannot help seeking. But the man who looks for a lie in everything, and becomes a willing friend to unhappiness, shall have a marvellous disillusioning: there hovers near him something unutterable, of which truth and happiness are but idolatrous images born of the night; the earth loses her dragging weight, the events and powers of earth become as a dream, and a gradual clearness widens round him like a summer evening. It is as though the beholder of these things began to wake, and it had only been the clouds of a passing dream that had been weaving about him. They will at some time disappear: and then will it be day.

5

But I have promised to speak of Schopenhauer, as far as my experience goes, as an *educator* and it is far from being sufficient to paint the ideal humanity which is the "Platonic idea" in Schopenhauer; especially as my representation is an imperfect one. The most difficult task remains; to say how a new circle of duties may spring from this ideal, and how one can reconcile such a transcendent aim with ordinary action; to prove, in short, that the ideal is *educative*. One might otherwise think it to be merely the blissful or intoxicating vision of a few rare moments, that leaves us afterwards the prey of a deeper disappointment. It is certain that the ideal begins to affect us in this way when we come suddenly to distinguish light and darkness, bliss and abhorrence; this is an experience that is as old as ideals themselves. But we ought not to stand in the doorway for long; we should soon leave the first stages, and ask the question, seriously and definitely, "Is it possible to bring that incredibly high aim so near us, that it should educate us, or 'lead us out' as well as lead us upward?"—in order that the great words of Goethe be not fulfilled in our case— "Man is born to a state of limitation: he can understand ends that are simple, present and definite, and is accustomed to make use of means that are near to his hand; but as soon as he comes into the open, he knows neither what he wishes nor what he ought to do, and it is all one whether he be confused by the multitude of objects or set beside himself by their greatness and importance. It is always his misfortune to be led to strive after something which he cannot attain by any ordinary activity of his own." The objection can be made with apparent reason against Schopenhauer's man, that his greatness and dignity can only turn our heads, and put us beyond all community with the active men of the world: the common round of duties, the noiseless tenor of life has disappeared. One man may possibly get accustomed to living in a reluctant dualism, that is, in a contradiction with himself;—becoming unstable, daily weaker and less productive:—while another will renounce all action on principle, and scarcely endure to see others active. The danger is always great when a man is too heavy-laden, and cannot really *accomplish* any duties. Stronger natures may be broken by it; the weaker, which are the majority, sink into a speculative laziness, and at last, from their laziness, lose even the power of speculation.

With regard to such objections, I will admit that our work has hardly begun, and so far as I know, I only see one thing clearly and definitely—that it is possible for that ideal picture to provide you and me with a chain of duties that may be accomplished; and some of us already feel its pressure. In order, however, to be able to speak in plain language of the formula under which I may gather the new circle of duties, I must begin with the following considerations.

The deeper minds of all ages have had pity for animals, because they suffer from life and have not the power to turn the sting of the suffering against themselves, and understand their being metaphysically. The sight of blind suffering is the spring of the deepest emotion. And in many quarters of the earth men have supposed that the souls of the guilty have entered into beasts, and that the blind suffering which at first sight calls for such pity has a clear meaning and purpose to the divine justice,—of punishment and atonement: and a heavy punishment it is, to be condemned to live in hunger and need, in the shape of a beast, and to reach no consciousness of one's self in this life. I can think of no harder lot than the wild beast's; he is driven to the forest by the fierce pang of hunger, that seldom leaves him at peace; and peace is itself a torment, the surfeit after horrid food, won, maybe, by a deadly fight with other animals. To cling to life, blindly and madly, with no other aim, to be ignorant of the reason, or even the fact, of one's punishment, nay, to thirst after it as if it were a pleasure, with all the perverted desire of a fool—this is what it means to be an animal. If universal nature leads up to man, it is to show us that he is necessary to redeem her from the curse of the beast's life, and that in him existence can find a mirror of itself wherein life appears, no longer blind, but in its real metaphysical significance. But we should consider where the beast ends and the man begins— the man, the one concern of Nature. As long as any one desires life as a pleasure in itself, he has not raised his eyes above the horizon of the beast; he only desires more consciously what the beast seeks by a blind impulse. It is so with us all, for the greater part of our lives. We do not shake off the beast, but are beasts ourselves, suffering we know not what.

But there are moments when we do know; and then the clouds break, and we see how, with the rest of nature, we are straining towards the man, as to something that stands high above us. We look round and behind us, and fear the sudden rush of light; the beasts are transfigured, and ourselves with them. The enormous migrations of mankind in the wildernesses of the world, the cities they found and the wars they wage, their ceaseless gatherings and dispersions and fusions, the doctrines they blindly follow, their mutual frauds and deceits, the cry of distress, the shriek of victory—are all a continuation of the beast in us: as if the education of man has been intentionally set back, and his promise of self-consciousness frustrated; as if, in fact, after yearning for man so long, and at last reaching him by her labour, Nature should now recoil from him and wish to return to a state of unconscious instinct. Ah! she has need of knowledge, and shrinks before the very knowledge she needs: the flame flickers unsteadily and fears its own brightness, and takes hold of a thousand things before the one thing for which knowledge is necessary. There are moments when we all know that our most elaborate arrangements are only designed to give us refuge from our real task in life; we wish to hide our heads somewhere, as if our Argus-eyed conscience could not find us out; we are quick to send our hearts on state-service, or money-making, or social duties, or scientific work, in order to possess them no longer ourselves; we are more willing and instinctive slaves of the hard day's work than mere living requires, because it seems to us more necessary not to be in a position to think. The hurry is universal, because every one is fleeing before himself; its concealment is just as universal, as we wish to seem contented and hide our wretchedness from the keener eyes; and so there is a common need for a new carillon of words to hang in the temple of life, and peal for its noisy festival. We all know the curious way in which unpleasant memories suddenly throng on us, and how we do our best by loud talk and violent gestures to put them out of our minds; but the gestures and the talk of our ordinary life make one think we are all in this condition, frightened of any memory or any inward gaze. What is it that is always troubling us? what is the gnat that will not let us sleep ? There are spirits all about us, each moment of life has something to say to us, but we will not listen to the spirit-voices. When we are quiet and alone, we fear that something will be whispered in our ears, and so we hate the quiet, and dull our senses in society.

We understand this sometimes, as I say, and stand amazed at the whirl and the rush and the anxiety and all the dream that we call our life; we seem to fear the awakening, and our dreams too become vivid and restless, as the awakening draws near. But we feel as well that we are too weak to endure long those intimate moments, and that we are not the men to whom universal nature looks as her redeemers. It is something to be able to raise our heads but for a moment and see the stream in which we are sunk so deep. We cannot gain even this transitory moment of awakening by our own strength; we must be lifted up—and who are they that will uplift us?

The sincere men who have cast out the beast, the philosophers, artists and saints. Nature—*quæ nunquam facit saltum*—has made her one leap in creating them; a leap of joy, as she feels herself for the first time at her goal, where she begins to see that she must learn not to have goals above her, and that she has played the game of transition too long. The knowledge transfigures her, and there rests on her face the gentle weariness of evening that men call "beauty." Her words after this transfiguration are as a great light shed over existence: and the highest wish that mortals can reach is to listen continually to her voice with ears that hear. If a man think of all that Schopenhauer, for example, must have *heard* in his life, he may well say to himself—"The deaf ears, the feeble understanding and shrunken heart, everything that I call mine, how I despise them! Not to be able to fly but only to flutter one's wings! To look above one's self and have no power to rise! To know the road that leads to the wide vision of the philosopher, and to reel back after a few steps! Were there but one day when the great wish might be fulfilled, how gladly would we pay for it with the rest of life! To rise as high as any thinker yet into the pure icy air of the mountain, where there are no mists and veils, and the inner constitution of things is shown in a stark and piercing clarity! Even by thinking of this the soul becomes infinitely alone; but were its wish fulfilled, did its glance once fall straight as a ray of light on the things below, were shame and anxiety and desire gone for ever—one could find no words for its state then, for the mystic and tranquil emotion with which, like the soul of Schopenhauer, it would look down on the monstrous hieroglyphics of existence and the petrified doctrines of "becoming"; not as the brooding night, but as the red and glowing day that streams over the earth. And what a destiny it is only to know enough of the fixity and happiness of the philosopher to feel the complete unfixity and unhappiness of the false philosopher, 'who without hope lives in desire': to know one's self to be the fruit of a tree that is too much in the shade ever to ripen, and to see a world of sunshine in front, where one may not go!"

There were sorrow enough here, if ever, to make such a man envious and spiteful: but he will turn aside, that he may not destroy his soul by a vain aspiration; and will discover a new circle of duties.

I can now give an answer to the question whether it be possible to approach the great ideal of Schopenhauer's man "by any ordinary activity of our own." In the first place, the new duties are certainly not those of a hermit; they imply rather a vast community, held together not by external forms but by a fundamental idea, namely that of *culture*; though only so far as it can put a single task before each of us—to bring the philosopher, the artist and the saint, within and without us, to the light, and to strive thereby for the completion of Nature. For Nature needs the artist, as she needs the philosopher, for a metaphysical end, the explanation of herself, whereby she may have a clear and sharp picture of what she only saw dimly in the troubled period of transition,—and so may reach self-consciousness. Goethe, in an arrogant yet profound phrase, showed how all Nature's attempts only have value in so far as the artist interprets her stammering words, meets her half-way, and speaks aloud what she really means. "I have often said, and will often repeat," he exclaims in one place, "the *causa finalis* of natural and human activity is dramatic poetry. Otherwise the stuff is of no use at all."

Finally, Nature needs the saint. In him the ego has melted away, and the suffering of his life is, practically, no longer felt as individual, but as the spring of the deepest sympathy and intimacy with all living creatures: he sees the wonderful transformation scene that the comedy of "becoming" never reaches, the attainment, at length, of the high state of man after which all nature is striving, that she may be delivered from herself. Without doubt, we all stand in close relation to him, as well as to the philosopher and the artist: there are moments, sparks from the clear fire of love, in whose light we understand the word "I" no longer; there is something beyond our being that comes, for those moments, to the hither side of it: and this is why we long in our hearts for a bridge from here to there. In our ordinary state we can do nothing towards the production of the new redeemer, and so we hate ourselves in this state with a hatred that is the root of the pessimism which Schopenhauer had to teach again to our age, though it is as old as the aspiration after culture.—Its root, not its flower; the foundation, not the summit; the beginning of the road, not the end: for we have to learn at some time to hate something else, more universal than our own personality with its wretched limitation, its change and its unrest—and this will be when we shall learn to love something else than we can love now. When we are ourselves received into that high order of philosophers, artists and saints, in this life or a reincarnation of it, a new object for our love and hate will also rise before us. As it is, we have our task and our circle of duties, our hates and our loves. For we know that culture requires us to make ready for the coming of the Schopenhauer man;—and this is the "use" we are to make of him;—we must know what obstacles there are and strike them from our path—in fact, wage unceasing war against everything that hindered our fulfilment, and prevented us from becoming Schopenhauer's men ourselves.

6

It is sometimes harder to agree to a thing than to understand it; many will feel this when they consider the proposition—"Mankind must toil unceasingly to bring forth individual great men: this and nothing else is its task." One would like to apply to society and its ends a fact that holds universally in the animal and vegetable world; where progress depends only on the higher individual types, which are rarer, yet more persistent, complex and productive. But traditional notions of what the end of society is, absolutely bar the way. We can easily understand how in the natural world, where one species passes at some point into a higher one, the aim of their evolution cannot be held to lie in the high level attained by the mass, or in the latest types developed;—but rather in what seem accidental beings produced here and there by favourable circumstances. It should be just as easy to understand that it is the duty of mankind to provide the circumstances favourable to the birth of the new redeemer, simply because men can have a consciousness of their object. But there is always something to prevent them. They find their ultimate aim in the happiness of all, or the greatest number, or in the expansion of a great commonwealth. A man will very readily decide to sacrifice his life for the state; he will be much slower to respond if an individual, and not a state, ask for the sacrifice. It seems to be out of reason that one man should exist for the sake of another : "Let it be rather for the sake of every other, or, at any rate, of as many as possible!" O upright judge! As if it were more in reason to let the majority decide a question of value and significance! For the problem is—"In what way may your life, the individual life, retain the highest value and the deepest significance? and how may it least be squandered? "Only by your living for the good of the rarest and most valuable types, not for that of the majority,—who are the most worthless types, taken as individuals. This way of thinking should be implanted and fostered in every young man's mind: he should regard himself both as a failure of Nature's handiwork and a testimony to her larger ideas. "She has succeeded badly," he should say; "but I will do honour to her great idea by being a means to its better success."

With these thoughts he will enter the circle of culture, which is the child of every man's self-knowledge and dissatisfaction. He will approach and say aloud: "I see something above me, higher and more human than I: let all help me to reach it, as I will help all who know and suffer as I do, that the man may arise at last who feels his knowledge and love, vision and power, to be complete and boundless, who in his universality is one with nature, the critic and judge of existence." It is difficult to give any one this courageous self-consciousness, because it is impossible to teach love; from love alone the soul gains, not only the clear vision that leads to self-contempt, but also the desire to look to a higher self which is yet hidden, and strive upward to it with all its strength. And so he who rests his hope on a future great man, receives his first "initiation into culture." The sign of this is shame or vexation at one's self, a hatred of one's own narrowness, a sympathy with the genius that ever raises its head again from our misty wastes, a feeling for all that is struggling into life, the conviction that Nature must be helped in her hour of need to press forward to the man, however ill she seem to prosper, whatever success may attend her marvellous forms and projects : so that the men with whom we live are like the debris of some precious sculptures, which cry out— "Come and help us! Put us together, for we long to become complete."

I called this inward condition the "first initiation into culture." I have now to describe the effects of the "second initiation," a task of greater difficulty. It is the passage from the inner life to the criticism of the outer life. The eye must be turned to find in the great world of movement the desire for culture that is known from the immediate experience of the individual; who must use his own strivings and aspirations as the alphabet to interpret those of humanity. He cannot rest here either, but must go higher. Culture demands from him not only that inner experience, not only the criticism of the outer world surrounding him, but action too to crown them all, the fight for culture against the influences and conventions and institutions where he cannot find his own aim,—the production of genius.

Any one who can reach the second step, will see how extremely rare and imperceptible the knowledge of that end is, though all men busy themselves with culture and expend vast labour in her service. He asks himself in amazement— "Is not such knowledge, after all, absolutely necessary? Can Nature be said to attain her end, if men have a false idea of the aim of their own labour?" And any one who thinks a great deal of Nature's unconscious adaptation of means to ends, will probably answer at once: "Yes, men may think and speak what they like about their ultimate end, their blind instinct will tell them the right road." It requires some experience of life to be able to contradict this: but let a man be convinced of the real aim of culture— the production of the true man and nothing else; let him consider that amid all the pageantry and ostentation of culture at the present time the conditions for his production are nothing but a continual "battle of the beasts": and he will see that there is great need for a conscious will to take the place of that blind instinct. There is another reason also;—to prevent the possibility of turning this obscure impulse to quite different ends, in a direction where our highest aim can no longer be attained. For we must beware of a certain kind of misapplied and parasitical culture; the powers at present most active in its propagation have other casts of thought that prevent their relation to culture from being pure and disinterested.

The first of these is the self-interest of the business men. This needs the help of culture, and helps her in return, though at the price of prescribing her ends and limits. And their favourite sorites is: "We must have as much knowledge and education as possible; this implies as great a need as possible for it, this again as much production, this again as much material wealth and happiness as possible."—This is the seductive formula. Its preachers would define education as the insight that makes man through and through a "child of his age" in his desires and their satisfaction, and gives him command over the best means of making money. Its aim would be to make "current" men, in the same sense as one speaks of the "currency" in money ; and in their view, the more "current" men there are, the happier the people. The object of modern educational systems is therefore to make each man as "current" as his nature will allow him, and to give him the opportunity for the greatest amount of success and happiness that can be got from his particular stock of knowledge. He is required to have just so much idea of his own value (through his liberal education) as to know what he can ask of life; and he is assured that a natural and necessary connection between "intelligence and property" not only exists, but is also a *moral* necessity. All education is detested that makes for loneliness, and has an aim above money-making, and requires a long time: men look askance on such serious education, as mere "refined egoism" or "immoral Epicureanism." The converse of course holds, according to the ordinary morality, that education must be soon over to allow the pursuit of money to be soon begun, and should be just thorough enough to allow of much money being made. The amount of education is determined by commercial interests. In short, "man has a necessary claim to worldly happiness; only for that reason is education necessary."

There is, secondly, the self-interest of the state, which requires the greatest possible breadth and universality of culture, and has the most effective weapons to carry out its wishes. If it be firmly enough established not only to initiate but control education and bear its whole weight, such breadth will merely profit the competition of the state with other states. A "highly civilised state "generally implies, at the present time, the task of setting free the spiritual forces of a generation just so far as they may be of use to the existing institutions,—as a mountain stream is split up by embankments and channels, and its diminished power made to drive mill-wheels, its full strength being more dangerous than useful to the mills. And thus "setting free" comes to mean rather "chaining up." Compare, for example, what the self-interest of the state has done for Christianity. Christianity is one of the purest manifestations of the impulse towards culture and the production of the saint: but being used in countless ways to turn the mills of the state authorities, it gradually became sick at heart, hypocritical and degenerate, and in antagonism with its original aim. Its last phase, the German Reformation, would have been nothing but a sudden flickering of its dying flame, had it not taken new strength and light from the clash and conflagration of states.

In the third place, culture will be favoured by all those people who know their own character to be offensive or tiresome, and wish to draw a veil of so-called "good form" over them. Words, gestures, dress, etiquette, and such external things, are meant to produce a false impression, the inner side to be judged from the outer. I sometimes think that modern men are eternally bored with each other and look to the arts to make them interesting. They let their artists make savoury and inviting dishes of them; they steep themselves in the spices of the East and West, and have a very interesting aroma after it all. They are ready to suit all palates: and every one will be served, whether he want something with a good or bad taste, something sublime or coarse, Greek or Chinese, tragedy or gutter-drama. The most celebrated chefs among the moderns who wish to interest and be interested at any price, are the French the worst are the Germans. This is really more comforting for the latter, and we have no reason to mind the French despising us for our want of interest, elegance and politeness, and being reminded of the Indian who longs for a ring through his nose, and then proceeds to tattoo himself.

Here I must digress a little. Many things in Germany have evidently been altered since the late war with France, and new requirements for German culture brought over. The war was for many their first venture into the more elegant half of the world: and what an admirable simplicity the conqueror shows in not scorning to learn something of culture from the conquered! The applied arts especially will be reformed to emulate our more refined neighbours, the German house furnished like the French, a "sound taste" applied to the German language by means of an Academy on the French model, to shake off the doubtful influence of Goethe—this is the judgment of our new Berlin Academician, Dubois-Raymond. Our theatres have been gradually moving, in a dignified way, towards the same goal, even the elegant German savant is now discovered—and we must now expect everything that does not conform to this law of elegance, our music, tragedy and philosophy to be thrust aside as un-German. But there were no need to raise a ringer for German culture, did German culture (which the Germans have yet to find) mean nothing but the little amenities that make life more decorative—including the arts of the dancing-master and the upholsterer;—or were they merely interested in academic rules of language and a general atmosphere of politeness. The late war and the self-comparison with the French do not seem to have aroused any further desires, and I suspect that the German has a strong wish for the moment to be free of the old obligations laid on him by his wonderful gifts of seriousness and profundity. He would much rather play the buffoon and the monkey, and learn the arts that make life amusing. But the German spirit cannot be more dishonoured than by being treated as wax for any elegant mould.

And if, unfortunately, a good many Germans will allow themselves to be thus moulded, one must continually say to them, till at last they listen:—"The old German way is no longer yours: it was hard, rough, and full of resistance; but it is still the most valuable material—one which only the greatest modellers can work with, for they alone are worthy to use it, What you have in you now is a soft pulpy stuff: make what you will out of it,—elegant dolls and interesting idols—Richard Wagner's phrase will still hold good, 'The German is awkward and ungainly when he wishes to be polite; he is high above all others, when he begins to take fire.'" All the elegant people have reason to beware of this German fire; it may one day devour them with all their wax dolls and idols. The prevailing love of "good form" in Germany may have a deeper cause in the breathless seizing at what the moment can give, the haste that plucks the fruit too green, the race and the struggle that cut the furrows in men's brows and stamp the same mark on all their actions. As if there were a poison in them that would not let them breathe, they rush about in disorder, anxious slaves of the "three m's," the moment, the mode and the mob: they see too well their want of dignity and fitness, and need a false elegance to hide their galloping consumption. The fashionable desire of "good form" is bound up with a loathing of man's inner nature : the one is to conceal, the other to be concealed. Education means now the concealment of man's misery and wickedness, his wild-beast quarrels, his eternal greed, his shamelessness in fruition. In pointing out the absence of a German culture, I have often had the reproach flung at me: "This absence is quite natural, for the Germans have been too poor and modest up to now. Once rich and conscious of themselves, our people will have a culture too." Faith may often produce happiness, yet *this* particular faith makes me unhappy, for I feel that the culture whose future raises such hopes—the culture of riches, politeness, and elegant concealments—is the bitterest foe of that German culture in which I believe. Every one who has to live among Germans suffers from the dreadful grayness and apathy of their lives, their formlessness, torpor and clumsiness, still more their envy, secretiveness and impurity: he is troubled by their innate love of the false and the ignoble, their wretched mimicry and translation of a good foreign thing into a bad German one. But now that the feverish unrest, the quest of gain and success, the intense prizing of the moment, is added to it all, it makes one furious to think that all this sickness can never be cured, but only painted over, by such a "cult of the interesting." And this among a people that has produced a Schopenhauer and a Wagner! and will produce others, unless we are blindly deceiving ourselves; for should not their very existence be a guarantee that such forces are even now potential in the German spirit? Or will they be exceptions, the last inheritors of the qualities that were once called German? I can see nothing to help me here, and return to my main argument again, from which my doubts and anxieties have made me digress. I have not yet enumerated all the forces that help culture without recognising its end, the production of genius. Three have been named; the self-interest of business, of the state, and of those who draw the cloak of "good form" over them. There is fourthly the self-interest of science, and the peculiar nature of her servants—the learned.

Science has the same relation to wisdom as current morality to holiness: she is cold and dry, loveless, and ignorant of any deep feeling of dissatisfaction and yearning. She injures her servants in helping herself, for she impresses her own character on them and dries up their humanity. As long as we actually mean by culture the progress of science, she will pass by the great suffering man and harden her heart, for science only sees the problems of knowledge, and suffering is something alien and unintelligible to her world—though no less a problem for that!

If one accustom himself to put down every experience in a dialectical form of question and answer, and translate it into the language of "pure reason," he will soon wither up and rattle his bones like a skeleton. We all know it: and why is it that the young do not shudder at these skeletons of men, but give themselves blindly to science without motive or measure? It cannot be the so-called "impulse to truth": for how could there be an impulse towards a pure, cold and objectless knowledge? The unprejudiced eye can see the real driving forces only too plainly. The vivisection of the professor has much to recommend it, as he himself is accustomed to finger and analyse all things—even the worthiest! To speak honestly, the savant is a complex of very various impulses and attractive forces he is a base metal throughout.

Take first a strong and increasing desire for intellectual adventure, the attraction of the new and rare as against the old and tedious. Add to that a certain joy in nosing the trail of dialectic, and beating the cover where the old fox,

Thought, lies hid; the desire is not so much for truth as the chase of truth, and the chief pleasure is in surrounding and artistically killing it. Add thirdly a love of contradiction whereby the personality is able to assert itself against all others: the battle's the thing, and the personal victory its aim,—truth only its pretext. The impulse to discover "particular truths" plays a great part in the professor, coming from his submission to definite ruling persons, classes, opinions, churches, governments, for he feels it a profit to himself to bring truth to their side.

The following characteristics of the savant are less common, but still found.—Firstly, downrightness and a feeling for simplicity, very valuable if more than a mere awkwardness and inability to deceive, deception requiring some mother-wit.—(Actually, we may be on our guard against too obvious cleverness and resource, and doubt the man's sincerity.)—Otherwise this downrightness is generally of little value, and rarely of any use to knowledge, as it follows tradition and speaks the truth only in "adiaphora"; it being lazier to speak the truth here than ignore it. Everything new means something to be unlearnt, and your downright man will respect the ancient dogmas and accuse the new evangelist of failing in the *sensus recti*. There was a similar opposition, with probability and custom on its side, to the theory of Copernicus. The professor's frequent hatred of philosophy is principally a hatred of the long trains of reasoning and artificiality of the proofs. Ultimately the savants of every age have a fixed limit; beyond which ingenuity is not allowed, and everything suspected as a conspirator against honesty.

Secondly, a clear vision of near objects, combined with great shortsightedness for the distant and universal. The professor's range is generally very small, and his eye must be kept close to the object. To pass from a point already considered to another, he has to move his whole optical apparatus. He cuts a picture into small sections, like a man using an opera-glass in the theatre, and sees now a head, now a bit of the dress, but nothing as a whole. The single sections are never combined for him, he only infers their connection, and consequently has no strong general impression. He judges a literary work, for example, by certain paragraphs or sentences or errors, as he can do nothing more; he will be driven to see in an oil painting nothing but a mass of daubs.

Thirdly, a sober conventionality in his likes and dislikes. Thus he especially delights in history because he can put his own motives into the actions of the past. A mole is most comfortable in a mole-hill. He is on his guard against all ingenious and extravagant hypotheses; but digs up industriously all the commonplace motives of the past, because he feels in sympathy with them. He is generally quite incapable of understanding and valuing the rare or the uncommon, the great or the real.

Fourthly, a lack of feeling, which makes him capable of vivisection. He knows nothing of the suffering that brings knowledge, and does not fear to tread where other men shudder. He is cold and may easily appear cruel. He is thought courageous, but he is not,—any more than the mule who does not feel giddiness.

Fifthly, diffidence, or a low estimate of himself. Though he live in a miserable alley of the world, he has no sense of sacrifice or surrender; he appears often to know in his inmost heart that he is not a flying but a crawling creature. And this makes him seem even pathetic.

Sixthly, loyalty to his teachers and leaders. From his heart he wishes to help them, and knows he can do it best with the truth. He has a grateful disposition, for he has only gained admittance through them to the high hall of science; he would never have entered by his own road. Any man to-day who can throw open a new province where his lesser disciples can work to some purpose, is famous at once; so great is the crowd that presses after him. These grateful pupils are certainly a misfortune to their teacher, as they all imitate him; his faults are exaggerated in their small persons, his virtues correspondingly diminished.

Seventhly, he will follow the usual road of all the professors, where a feeling for truth springs from a lack of ideas, and the wheel once started goes on. Such natures become compilers, commentators, makers of indices and herbaria; they rummage about one special department because they have never thought there are others. Their industry has something of the monstrous stupidity of gravitation; and so they can often bring their labours to an end.

Eighthly, a dread of ennui. While the true thinker desires nothing more than leisure, the professor fears it, not knowing how it is to be used. Books are his comfort; he listens to everybody's different thoughts and keeps himself amused all day. He especially chooses books with a personal relation to himself, that make him feel some emotion of like or dislike; books that have to do with himself or his position, his political, aesthetic, or even grammatical doctrines; if he have mastered even one branch of knowledge, the means to flap away the flies of ennui will not fail him.

Ninthly, the motive of the bread-winner, the "cry of the empty stomach," in fact. Truth is used as a direct means of preferment, when she can be attained; or as a way to the good graces of the fountains of honour—and bread. Only, however, in the sense of the "particular truth": there is a gulf between the profitable truths that many serve, and the unprofitable truths to which only those few people devote themselves whose motto is not *ingenii largitor venter*.

Tenthly, a reverence for their fellow-professors and a fear of their displeasure—a higher and rarer motive than the last, though not uncommon. All the members of the guild are jealously on guard, that the truth which means so much bread and honour and position may really be baptized in the name of its discoverer. The one pays the other reverence for the truth he has found, in order to exact the toll again if he should find one himself. The Untruth, the Error is loudly exploded, that the workers may not be too many; here and there the real truth will be exploded to let a few bold and stiff-necked errors be on show for a time; there is never a lack of "moral idiosyncrasies,"—formerly called rascalities.

Eleventhly, the "savant for vanity," now rather rare. He will get a department for himself somehow, and investigate curiosities, especially if they demand unusual expenditure, travel, research, or communication with all parts of the world. He is quite satisfied with the honour of being regarded as a curiosity himself, and never dreams of earning a living by his erudite studies.

Twelfthly, the "savant for amusement." He loves to look for knots in knowledge and to untie them; not too energetically however, lest he lose the spirit of the game. Thus he does not penetrate the depths, though he often observes something that the microscopic eyes of the bread-and-butter scientist never see.

If I speak, lastly, of the "impulse towards justice" as a further motive of the savant, I may be answered that this noble impulse, being metaphysical in its nature, is too indistinguishable from the rest, and really incomprehensible to mortal mind; and so I leave the thirteenth heading with the pious wish that the impulse may be less rare in the professor than it seems. For a spark in his soul from the fire of justice is sufficient to irradiate and purify it, so that he can rest no more and is driven for ever from the cold or lukewarm condition in which most of his fellows do their daily work.

All these elements, or a part of them, must be regarded as fused and pounded together, to form the Servant of Truth. For the sake of an absolutely inhuman thing—mere purposeless, and therefore motiveless, knowledge—a mass of very human little motives have been chemically combined, and as the result we have the professor,—so transfigured in the light of that pure unearthly object that the mixing and pounding which went to form him are all forgotten! It is very curious. Yet there are moments when they must be remembered,—when we have to think of the professor's significance to culture. Any one with observation can see that he is in his essence and by his origin unproductive, and has a natural hatred of the productive; and thus there is an endless feud between the genius and the savant in idea and practice. The latter wishes to kill Nature by analysing and comprehending it, the former to increase it by a new living Nature. The happy age does not need or know the savant; the sick and sluggish time ranks him as its highest and worthiest.

Who were physician enough to know the health or sickness of our time? It is clear that the professor is valued too highly, with evil consequences for the future genius, for whom he has no compassion, merely a cold, contemptuous criticism, a shrug of the shoulders, as if at something strange and perverted for which he has neither time nor inclination. And so he too knows nothing of the aim of culture.

In fact, all these considerations go to prove that the aim of culture is most unknown precisely where the interest in it seems liveliest. The state may trumpet as it will its services to culture, it merely helps culture in order to help itself, and does not comprehend an aim that stands higher than its own well-being or even existence. The business men in their continual demand for education merely wish for—business. When the pioneers of "good form" pretend to be the real helpers of culture, imagining that all art, for example, is merely to serve their own needs, they are clearly affirming themselves in affirming culture. Of the savant enough has already been said. All four are emulously thinking how they can benefit *themselves* with the help of culture, but have no thoughts at all when their own interests are not engaged. And so they have done nothing to improve the conditions for the birth of genius in modern times; and the opposition to original men has grown so far that no Socrates could ever live among us, and certainly could never reach the age of seventy.

I remember saying in the third chapter that our whole modern world was not so stable that one could prophesy an eternal life to its conception of culture. It is likely that the next millennium may reach two or three new ideas that might well make the hair of our present generation stand on end. The belief in the metaphysical significance of culture would not be such a horrifying thing, but its effects on educational methods might be so.

It requires a totally new attitude of mind to be able to, look away from the present educational institutions to the strangely different ones that will be necessary for the second or third generation, At present the labours of higher education produce merely the savant or the official or the business man or the Philistine or, more commonly, a mixture of all four; and the future institutions will have a harder task;—not in itself harder, as it is really more natural, and so easier; and further, could anything be harder than to make a youth into a savant against nature, as now happens?—But the difficulty lies in unlearning what we know and setting up a new aim; it will be an endless trouble to change the fundamental idea of our present educational system, that has its roots in the Middle Ages and regards the mediaeval savant as the ideal type of culture. It is already time to put these objects before us; for some generation must begin the battle, of which a later generation will reap the victory. The solitary man who has understood the new fundamental idea of culture is at the parting of the ways; on the one he will be welcomed by his age, laurels and rewards will be his, powerful parties will uphold him, he will have as many in sympathy behind him as in front, and when the leader speaks the word of deliverance, it will echo through all the ranks. The first duty is to "fight in line," the second to treat as foes all who will not "fall in." On the other way he will find fewer companions; it is steeper and more tortuous. The travellers on the first road laugh at him, as his way is the more troublesome and dangerous; and they try to entice him over. If the two ways cross, he is ill-treated, cast aside or left alone. What significance has any particular form of culture for these several travellers? The enormous throng that press to their end on the first road, understand by it the laws and institutions that enable them to go forward in regular fashion and rule out all the solitary and obstinate people who look towards higher and remoter objects. To the small company on the other road it has quite a different office: they wish to guard themselves, by means of a strong organisation, from being swept away by the throng, to prevent their individual members from fainting on the way or turning in spirit from their great task. These solitary men must finish their work; that is why they should all hold together; and those who have their part in the scheme will take thought to prepare themselves with ever-increasing purity of aim for the birth of the genius, and ensure that the time be ripe for him. Many are destined to help on the labour, even among the second-rate talents, and it is only in submission to such a destiny that they can feel they are living for a duty, and have a meaning and an object in their lives. But at present these talents are being turned from the road their instinct has chosen by the seductive tones of the "fashionable culture," that plays on their selfish side, their vanities and weaknesses; and the time-spirit ever whispers in their ears its flattering counsel:—"Follow me and go not thither! There you are only servants and tools, overshadowed by higher natures with no scope for your own, drawn by threads, hung with fetters, slaves and automatons. With me you may enjoy your true personality, and be masters, your talents may shine with their own light, and yourselves stand in the front ranks with an immense following round you; and the acclamation of public opinion will rejoice you more than a wandering breath of approval sent down from the cold ethereal heights of genius." Even the best men are snared by such allurements, and the ultimate difference comes not so much from the rarity and power of their talent, as the influence of a certain heroic disposition at the base of them, and an inner feeling of kinship with genius. For there are men who feel it as their own misery when they see the genius in painful toil and struggle, in danger of self-destruction, or neglected by the short-sighted selfishness of the state, the superficiality of the business men, and the cold arrogance of the professors; and I hope there may be some to understand what I mean by my sketch of Schopenhauer's destiny, and to what end Schopenhauer can really educate.

7

But setting aside all thoughts of any educational revolution in the distant future;—what provision is required *now*, that our future philosopher may have the best chance of opening his eyes to a life like Schopenhauer's—hard as it is, yet still livable? What, further, must be discovered that may make his influence on his contemporaries more certain? And what obstacles must be removed before his example can have its full effect and the philosopher train another philosopher? Here we descend to be practical.

Nature always desires the greatest utility, but does not understand how to find the best and handiest means to her end; that is her great sorrow, and the cause of her melancholy. The impulse towards her own redemption shows clearly her wish to give men a significant existence by the generation of the philosopher and the artist: but how unclear and weak is the effect she generally obtains with her artists and philosophers, and how seldom is there any effect at all ! She is especially perplexed in her efforts to make the philosopher useful; her methods are casual and tentative, her failures innumerable; most of her philosophers never touch the common good of mankind at all. Her actions seem those of a spendthrift; but the cause lies in no prodigal luxury, but in her inexperience. Were she human, she would probably never cease to be dissatisfied with herself and her bungling. Nature shoots the philosopher at mankind like an arrow; she. does not aim, but hopes that the arrow will stick somewhere. She makes countless mistakes, that give her pain. She is as extravagant in the sphere of culture as in her planting and sowing. She fulfils her ends in a large and clumsy fashion, using up far too much of her strength. The artist has the same relation to the connoisseurs and lovers of his art as a piece of heavy artillery to a flock of sparrows. It is a fool's part to use a great avalanche to sweep away a little snow, to kill a man in order to strike the fly on his nose. The artist and the philosopher are witnesses against Nature's adaptation of her means, however well they may show the wisdom of her ends. They only reach a few and should reach all—and even these few are not struck with the strength they used when they shot. It is sad to have to value art so differently as cause and effect; how huge in its inception, how faint the echo afterwards! The artist does his work as Nature bids him, for the benefit of other men no doubt of it; but he knows that none of those men will understand and love his work as he understands and loves it himself. That lonely height of love and understanding is necessary, by Nature's clumsy law, to produce a lower type; the great and noble are used as the means to the small and ignoble. Nature is a bad manager; her expenses are far greater than her profits: for all her riches she must one day go bankrupt. She would have acted more reasonably to make the rule of her household—small expense and hundredfold profit; if there had been, for example, only a few artists with moderate powers, but an immense number of hearers to appreciate them, stronger and more powerful characters than the artists themselves; then the effect of the art-work, in comparison with the cause, might be a hundred-tongued echo. One might at least expect cause and effect to be of equal power; but Nature lags infinitely behind this consummation. An artist, and especially a philosopher, seems often to have dropped by chance into his age, as a wandering hermit or straggler cut off from the main body. Think how utterly great Schopenhauer is, and what a small and absurd effect he has had! An honest man can feel no greater shame at the present time than at the thought of the casual treatment Schopenhauer has received and the evil powers that have up to now killed his effect among men. First there was the want of readers,—to the eternal shame of our cultivated age;—then the inadequacy of his first public adherents, as soon as he had any; further, I think, the crassness of the modern man towards books, which he will no longer take seriously. As an outcome of many attempts to adapt Schopenhauer to this enervated age, the new danger has gradually arisen of regarding him as an odd kind of pungent herb, of taking him in grains, as a sort of metaphysical pepper. In this way he has gradually become famous, and I should think more have heard his name than Hegel's; and, for all that, he is still a solitary being, who has failed of his effect.—Though the honour of causing the failure belongs least of all to the barking of his literary antagonists; first because there are few men with the patience to read them, and secondly, because any one who does, is sent immediately to Schopenhauer himself; for who will let a donkey-driver prevent him from mounting a fine horse, however much he praise his donkey?

Whoever has recognised Nature's unreason in our time, will have to consider some means to help her; his task will be to bring the free spirits and the sufferers from this age to know Schopenhauer; and make them tributaries to the flood that is to overbear all the clumsy uses to which Nature even now is accustomed to put her philosophers. Such men will see that the identical obstacles hinder the effect of a great philosophy and the production of the great philosopher; and so will direct their aims to prepare the regeneration of Schopenhauer, which means that of the philosophical genius. The real opposition to the further spread of his doctrine in the past, and the regeneration of the philosopher in the future, is the perversity of human nature as it is; and all the great men that are to be must spend infinite pains in freeing themselves from it. The world they enter is plastered over with pretence—including not merely religious dogmas, but such juggling conceptions as "progress," "universal education," "nationalism," "the modern state" ; practically all our general terms have an artificial veneer over them that will bring a clearer-sighted posterity to reproach our age bitterly for its warped and stunted growth, however loudly we may boast of our "health." The beauty of the antique vases, says Schopenhauer, lies in the simplicity with which they express their meaning and object; it is so with all the ancient implements; if Nature produced amphorae, lamps, tables, chairs, helmets, shields, breastplates and the like, they would resemble these. And, as a corollary, whoever considers how we all manage our art, politics, religion and education—to say nothing of our vases!—will find in them a barbaric exaggeration and arbitrariness of expression. Nothing is more unfavourable to the rise of genius than such monstrosities. They are unseen and undiscoverable, the leaden weights on his hand when he will set it to the plough; the weights are only shaken off with violence, and his highest work must to an extent always bear the mark of it.

In considering the conditions that, at best, keep the born philosopher from being oppressed by the perversity of the age, I am surprised to find they are partly those in which Schopenhauer himself grew up. True, there was no lack of opposing influences; the evil time drew perilously near him in the person of a vain and pretentious mother. But the proud republican character of his father rescued him from her and gave him the first quality of a philosopher—a rude and strong virility. His father was neither an official nor a savant; he travelled much abroad with his son,—a great help to one who must know men rather than books, and worship truth before the state. In time he got accustomed to national peculiarities: he made England, France and Italy equally his home, and felt no little sympathy with the

Spanish character. On the whole, he did not think it an honour to be born in Germany, and I am not sure that the new political conditions would have made him change his mind. He held quite openly the opinion that the state's one object was to give protection at home and abroad, and even protection against its "protectors," and to attribute any other object to it was to endanger its true end. And so, to the consternation of all the so-called liberals, he left his property to the survivors of the Prussian soldiers who fell in 1848 in the fight for order. To understand the state and its duties in this single sense may seem more and more henceforth the sign of intellectual superiority; for the man with the *furor philosophicus* in him will no longer have time for the *furor politicus* and will wisely keep from reading the newspapers or serving a party; though he will not hesitate a moment to take his place in the ranks if his country be in real need. All states are badly managed, when other men than politicians busy themselves with politics; and they deserve to be ruined by their political amateurs.

Schopenhauer had another great advantage—that he had never been educated for a professor, but worked for some time (though against his will) as a merchant's clerk, and through all his early years breathed the freer air of a great commercial house. A savant can never become a philosopher: Kant himself could not, but remained in a chrysalis stage to the end, in spite of the innate force of his genius. Any one who thinks I do Kant wrong in saying this does not know what a philosopher is—not only a great thinker, but also a real man; and how could a real man have sprung from a savant? He who lets conceptions, opinions, events, books come between himself and things, and is born for history (in the widest sense), will never see anything at once, and never be himself a thing to be "seen at once"; though both these powers should be in the philosopher, as he must take most of his doctrine from himself and be himself the copy and compendium of the whole world. If a man look at himself through a veil of other people's opinions, no wonder he sees nothing but—those opinions. And it is thus that the professors see and live. But Schopenhauer had the rare happiness of seeing the genius not only in himself, but also outside himself—in Goethe; and this double reflection taught him everything about the aims and culture of the learned. He knew by this experience how the free strong man, to whom all artistic culture was looking, must come to be born; and could he, after this vision, have much desire to busy himself with the so-called "art," in the learned, hypocritical manner of the moderns? He had seen something higher than that—an awful unearthly judgment-scene in which all life, even the highest and completest, was weighed and found too light; he had beheld the saint as the judge of existence. We cannot tell how early Schopenhauer reached this view of life, and came to hold it with such intensity as to make all his writings an attempt to mirror it; we know that the youth had this great vision, and can well believe it of the child. Everything that he gained later from life and books, from all the realms of knowledge, was only a means of colour and expression to him ; the Kantian philosophy itself was to him an extraordinary rhetorical instrument for making the utterance of his vision, as he thought, clearer; the Buddhist and Christian mythologies occasionally served the same end. He had one task and a thousand means to execute it; one meaning, and innumerable hieroglyphs to express it.

It was one of the high conditions of his existence that he really could live for such a task—according to his motto *vitam impendere vero*—and none of life's material needs could shake his resolution; and we know the splendid return he made his father for this. The contemplative man in Germany usually pursues his scientific studies to the detriment of his sincerity, as a "considerate fool," in search of place and honour, circumspect and obsequious, and fawning on his influential superiors. Nothing offended the savants more than Schopenhauer's unlikeness to them.

8

These are a few of the conditions under which the philosophical genius can at least come to light in our time, in spite of all thwarting influences;—a virility of character, an early knowledge of mankind, an absence of learned education and narrow patriotism, of compulsion to earn his livelihood or depend on the state,—freedom in fact, and again freedom; the same marvellous and dangerous element in which the Greek philosophers grew up. The man who will reproach him, as Niebuhr did Plato, with being a bad citizen, may do so, and be himself a good one; so he and Plato will be right together! Another may call this great freedom presumption; he is also right, as he could not himself use the freedom properly if he desired it, and would certainly presume too far with it. This freedom is really a grave burden of guilt; and can only be expiated by great actions. Every ordinary son of earth has the right of looking askance on such endowments; and may Providence keep him from being so endowed—burdened, that is, with such terrible duties! His freedom and his loneliness would be his ruin, and ennui would turn him into a fool, and a mischievous fool at that.

A father may possibly learn something from this that he may use for his son's private education, though one must not expect fathers to have only philosophers for their sons. It is possible that they will always oppose their sons becoming philosophers, and call it mere perversity; Socrates was sacrificed to the fathers' anger, for "corrupting the youth,' and Plato even thought a new ideal state necessary to prevent the philosophers' growth from being dependent on the fathers' folly. It looks at present as though Plato had really accomplished something; for the modern state counts the encouragement of philosophy as one of its duties and tries to secure for a number of men at a time the sort of freedom that conditions the philosopher. But, historically, Plato has been very unlucky; as soon as a structure has risen corresponding actually to his proposals, it has always turned, on a closer view, into a goblin-child, a monstrous changeling; compare the ecclesiastical state of the Middle Ages with the government of the "God-born king" of which Plato dreamed! The modern state is furthest removed from the idea of the Philosopher-king (Thank Heaven for that ! the Christian will say); but we must think whether it takes that very "encouragement of philosophy" in a Platonic sense, I mean as seriously and honestly as if its highest object were to produce more Platos. If the philosopher seem, as usual, an accident of his time, does the state make it its conscious business to turn the accidental into the necessary and help Nature here also?

Experience teaches us a better way—or a worse: it says that nothing so stands in the way of the birth and growth of Nature's philosopher as the bad philosophers made "by order." A poor obstacle, isn't it? and the same that Schopenhauer pointed out in his famous essay on University philosophy. I return to this point, as men must be forced to take it seriously, to be driven to activity by it; and I think all writing is useless that does not contain such a stimulus to activity. And anyhow it is a good thing to apply Schopenhauer's eternal theories once more to our own contemporaries, as some kindly soul might think that everything has changed for the better in Germany since his fierce diatribes. Unfortunately his work is incomplete on this side as well, unimportant as the side may be.

The "freedom" that the state, as I said, bestows on certain men for the sake of philosophy is, properly speaking, no freedom at all, but an office that maintains its holder. The "encouragement of philosophy" means that there are to-day a number of men whom the state enables to make their living out of philosophy; whereas the old sages of Greece were not paid by the state, but at best were presented, as Zeno was, with a golden crown and a monument in the Ceramicus. I cannot say generally whether truth is served by showing the way to live by her, since everything depends on the character of the individual who shows the way. I can imagine a degree of pride in a man saying to his fellow-men, "take care of me, as I have something better to do—namely to take care of you." We should not be angry at such a heightened mode of expression in Plato and Schopenhauer; and so they might properly have been University philosophers,—as Plato, for example, was a court philosopher for a while without lowering the dignity of philosophy. But in Kant we have the usual submissive professor, without any nobility in his relations with the state; and thus he could not justify the University philosophy when it was once assailed. If there be natures like Schopenhauer's and Plato's, which can justify it, I fear they will never have the chance, as the state would never venture to give such men these positions, for the simple reason that every state fears them, and will only favour philosophers it does not fear. The state obviously has a special fear of philosophy, and will try to attract more philosophers, to create the impression that it has philosophy on its side,—because it has those men on its side who have the title without the power. But if there should come one who really proposes to cut everything to the quick, the state included, with the knife of truth, the state, that affirms its own existence above all, is justified in banishing him as an enemy, just as it bans a religion that exalts itself to be its judge. The man who consents to be a state philosopher, must also consent to be regarded as renouncing the search for truth in all its secret retreats. At any rate, so long as he enjoys his position, he must recognise something higher than truth the state. And not only the state, but everything required by it for existence—a definite form of religion, a social system, a standing army; a *noli me tangere* is written above all these things. Can a University philosopher ever keep clearly before him the whole round of these duties and limitations? I do not know. The man who has done so and remains a state-official, is a false friend to truth; if he has not,—I think he is no friend to truth either. But general considerations like these are always the weakest in their influence on mankind. Most people will find it enough to shrug their shoulders and say, "As if anything great and pure has ever been able to maintain itself on this earth without some concession to human vulgarity! Would you rather the state persecuted philosophers than paid them for official services? "Without answering this last question, I will merely say that these "concessions" of philosophy to the state go rather far at present. In the first place, the state chooses its own philosophical servants, as many as its institutions require; it therefore pretends to be able to distinguish the good and the bad philosophers, and even assumes there must be a sufficient supply of good ones to fill all the chairs. The state is the authority not only for their goodness but their numbers. Secondly, it confines those it has chosen to a definite place and a definite activity among particular men; they must instruct every undergraduate who wants instruction, daily, at stated hours. The question is whether a philosopher can bind himself, with a good conscience, to have something to teach every day, to any one who wishes to listen. Must he not appear to know more than he does, and speak, before an unknown audience, of things that he could mention without risk only to his most intimate friends? And above all, does he not surrender the precious freedom of following his genius when and wherever it call him, by the mere fact of being bound to think at stated times on a fixed subject? And before young men, too! Is not such thinking in its nature emasculate? And suppose he felt some day that he had no ideas just then—and yet must be in his place and appear to be thinking What then?

"But," one will say, "he is not a thinker but mainly a depository of thought, a man of great learning in all previous philosophies. Of these he can always say something that his scholars do not know." This is actually the third, and the most dangerous, concession made by philosophy to the state, when it is compelled to appear in the form of erudition, as the knowledge (more specifically) of the history of philosophy. The genius looks purely and lovingly on existence, like a poet, and cannot dive too deep into it;—and nothing is more abhorrent to him than to burrow among the innumerable strange and wrong-headed opinions. The learned history of the past was never a true philosopher's business, in India or Greece; and a professor of philosophy who busies himself with such matters must be, at best, content to hear it said of him, "He is an able scholar, antiquary, philologist, historian,"—but never, "He is a philosopher." I said, "at best": for a scholar feels that most of the learned works written by University philosophers are badly done, without any real scientific power, and generally are dread- fully tedious. Who will blow aside, for example, the Lethean vapour with which the history of Greek philosophy has been enveloped by the dull though not very scientific works of Ritter, Brandis and Zeller? I, at any rate, would rather read Diogenes Laertius than Zeller, because at least the spirit of the old philosophers lives in Diogenes, but neither that nor any other spirit in Zeller. And, after all, what does the history of philosophy matter to our young men Are they to be discouraged by the welter of opinions from having any of their own; or taught to join the chorus that approves the vastness of our progress? Are they to learn to hate or perhaps despise philosophy? One might expect the last, knowing the torture the students endure for their philosophical examinations, in having to get into their unfortunate heads the maddest efforts of the human mind as well as the greatest and profoundest. The only method of criticising a philosophy that is possible and proves anything at all—namely to see whether one can live by it—has never been taught at the universities; only the criticism of words, and again words, is taught there. Imagine a young head, without much experience of life, being stuffed with fifty systems (in the form of words) and fifty criticisms of them, all mixed up together,—what an overgrown wilderness he will come to be, what contempt he will feel for a philosophical education! It is, of course, not an education in philosophy at all, but in the art of passing a philosophical examination: the usual result being the pious ejaculation of the wearied examinee, "Thank God I am no philosopher, but a Christian and a good citizen!"

What if this cry were the ultimate object of the state, and the "education" or leading to philosophy were merely a leading *from* philosophy? We may well ask.—But if so, there is one thing to fear—that the youth may some day find out to what end philosophy is thus mis-handled. "Is the highest thing of all, the production of the philosophical genius, nothing but a pretext, and the main object perhaps to hinder his production? And is Reason turned to Unreason?" Then woe to the whole machinery of political and professorial trickery!

Will it soon become notorious? I do not know; but anyhow university philosophy has fallen into a general state of doubting and despair. The cause lies partly in the feebleness of those who hold the chairs at present: and if Schopenhauer had to write his treatise on university philosophy to-day, he would find the club no longer necessary, but could conquer with a bulrush. They are the heirs and successors of those slip-shod thinkers whose crazy heads Schopenhauer struck at: their childish natures and dwarfish frames remind one of the Indian proverb: " men are born according to their deeds, deaf, dumb, misshapen." Those fathers deserved such sons, "according to their deeds," as the proverb says. Hence the students will, no doubt, soon get on without the philosophy taught at their university, just as those who are not university men manage to do without it already. This can be tested from one's own experience: in my student-days, for example, I found the university philosophers very ordinary men indeed, who had collected together a few conclusions from the other sciences, and in their leisure hours read the newspapers and went to concerts; they were treated by their academic colleagues with politely veiled contempt. They had the reputation of knowing very little, but of never being at a loss for obscure expressions to conceal their ignorance. They had a preference for those obscure regions where a man could not walk long with clear vision. One said of the natural sciences, "Not one of them can fully explain to me the origin of matter; then what do I care about them all?"— Another said of history, "It tells nothing new to the man with ideas": in fact, they always found reasons for its being more philosophical to know nothing than to learn anything. If they let themselves be drawn to learn, a secret instinct made them fly from the actual sciences and found a dim kingdom amid their gaps and uncertainties. They "led the way" in the sciences in the sense that the quarry "leads the way" for the hunters who are behind him. Recently they have amused themselves with asserting they are merely the watchers on the frontier of the sciences. The Kantian doctrine is of use to them here, and they industriously build up an empty scepticism on it, of which in a short time nobody will take any more notice. Here and there one will rise to a little metaphysic of his own, with the general accompaniment of headaches and giddiness and bleeding at the nose After the usual ill-success of their voyages into the clouds and the mist, some hard-headed young student of the real sciences will pluck them down by the skirts, and their faces will assume the expression now habitual to them, of offended dignity at being found out. They have lost their happy confidence, and not one of them will venture a step further for the sake of his philosophy. Some used to believe they could find out new religions or reinstate old ones by their systems. They have given up such pretensions now, and have become mostly mild, muddled folk, with no Lucretian boldness, but merely some spiteful complaints of the "dead weight that lies on the intellects of mankind"! No one can even learn logic from them now, and their obvious knowledge of their own powers has made them discontinue the dialectical disputations common in the old days. There is much more care and modesty, logic and inventiveness, in a word, more philosophical method in the work of the special sciences than in the so-called "philosophy," and every one will agree with the temperate words of Bagehot on the present system builders: "Unproved abstract principles without number have been eagerly caught up by sanguine men, and then carefully spun out into books and theories, which were to explain the whole world. But the world goes clear against these abstractions, and it must do so, as they require it to go in antagonistic directions. The mass of a system attracts the young and impresses the unwary; but cultivated people are very dubious about it. They are ready to receive hints and suggestions, and the smallest real truth is ever welcome. But a large book of deductive philosophy is much to be suspected. Who is not almost sure beforehand that the premises will contain a strange mixture of truth and error, and therefore that it will not be worth while to spend life in reasoning over their consequences?" The philosophers, especially in Germany, used to sink into such a state of abstraction that they were in continual danger of running their heads against a beam; but there is a whole herd of Laputan flappers about them to give them in time a gentle stroke on their eyes or anywhere else. Sometimes the blows are too hard; and then these scorners of earth forget themselves and strike back, but the victim always escapes them. " Fool, you do not see the beam," says the flapper; and often the philosopher does see the beam, and calms down. These flappers are the natural sciences and history; little by little they have so overawed the German dream-craft which has long taken the place of philosophy, that the dreamer would be only too glad to give up the attempt to run alone: but when they unexpectedly fall into the others' arms, or try to put leading-strings on them that they may be led themselves, those others flap as terribly as they can, as if they would say, "This is all that is wanting,—that a philosophaster like this should lay his impure hands on us, the natural sciences and history! Away with him!" Then they start back, knowing not where to turn or to ask the way. They wanted to have a little physical knowledge at their back, possibly in the form of empirical psychology (like the Herbartians), or perhaps a little history; and then they could at least make a public show of behaving scientifically, although in their hearts they may wish all philosophy and all science at the devil.

But granted that this herd of bad philosophers is ridiculous—and who will deny it?—how far are they also harmful? They are harmful just because they make philosophy ridiculous. As long as this imitation-thinking continues to be recognised by the state, the lasting effect of a true philosophy will be destroyed, or at any rate circumscribed; nothing does this so well as the curse of ridicule that the representatives of the great cause have drawn on them, for it attacks that cause itself. And so I think it will encourage culture to deprive philosophy of its political and academic standing, and relieve state and university of the task, impossible for them, of deciding between true and false philosophy. Let the philosophers run wild, forbid them any thoughts of office or civic position, hold them out no more bribes,—nay, rather persecute them and treat them ill,—you will see a wonderful result. They will flee in terror and seek a roof where they can, these poor phantasms; one will become a parson, another a schoolmaster, another will creep into an editorship, another write school-books for young ladies' colleges, the wisest of them will plough the fields, the vainest go to court. Everything will be left suddenly empty, the birds flown: for it is easy to get rid of bad philosophers,—one only has to cease paying them. And that is a better plan than the open patronage of any philosophy, whatever it be, for state reasons.

The state has never any concern with truth, but only with the truth useful to it, or rather, with anything that is useful to it, be it truth, half-truth, or error. A coalition between state and philosophy has only meaning when the latter can promise to be unconditionally useful to the state, to put its well-being higher than truth. It would certainly be a noble thing for the state to have truth as a paid servant; but it knows well enough that it is the essence of truth to be paid nothing and serve nothing. So the state's servant turns out to be merely "false truth," a masked actor who cannot perform the office required from the real truth—the affirmation of the state's worth and sanctity. When a mediaeval prince wished to be crowned by the Pope, but could not get him to consent, he appointed an antipope to do the business for him. This may serve up to a certain point ; but not when the modern state appoints an "anti-philosophy" to legitimise it; for it has true philosophy against it just as much as before, or even more so. I believe in all seriousness that it is to the state's advantage to have nothing further to do with philosophy, to demand nothing from it, and let it go its own way as much as possible. Without this indifferent attitude, philosophy may become dangerous and oppressive, and will have to be persecuted.—The only interest the state can have in the university lies in the training of obedient and useful citizens; and it should hesitate to put this obedience and usefulness in doubt by demanding an examination in philosophy from the young men. To make a bogey of philosophy may be an excellent way to frighten the idle and incompetent from its study; but this advantage is not enough to counterbalance the danger that this kind of compulsion may arouse from the side of the more reckless and turbulent spirits. They learn to know about forbidden books, begin to criticise their teachers, and finally come to understand the object of university philosophy and its examinations; not to speak of the doubts that may be fostered in the minds of young theologians, as a consequence of which they are beginning to be extinct in Germany, like the ibexes in the Tyrol.

I know the objections that the state could bring against all this, as long as the lovely Hegel-corn was yellowing in all the fields; but now that hail has destroyed the crop and all men's hopes of it, now that nothing has been fulfilled and all the barns are empty,—there are no more objections to be made, but rather rejections of philosophy itself. The state has now the power of rejection; in Hegel's time it only wished to have it—and that makes a great difference. The state needs no more the sanction of philosophy, and philosophy has thus become superfluous to it. It will find advantage in ceasing to maintain its professors, or (as I think will soon happen) in merely pretending to maintain them; but it is of still greater importance that the university should see the benefit of this as well. At least I believe the real sciences must see that their interest lies in freeing themselves from all contact with sham science. And further, the reputation of the universities hangs too much in the balance for them not to welcome a severance from methods that are thought little of even in academic circles. The outer world has good reason for its wide-spread contempt of universities; they are reproached with being cowardly, the small fearing the great, and the great fearing public opinion; it is said that they do not lead the higher thought of the age but hobble slowly behind it, and cleave no longer to the fundamental ideas of the recognised sciences. Grammar, for example, is studied more diligently than ever without any one seeing the necessity of a rigorous training in speech and writing. The gates of Indian antiquity are being opened, and the scholars have no more idea of the most imperishable works of the Indians—their philosophies—than a beast has of playing the harp; though Schopenhauer thinks that the acquaintance with Indian philosophy is one of the greatest advantages possessed by our century. Classical antiquity is the favourite playground nowadays, and its effect is no longer classical and formative; as is shown by the students, who are certainly no models for imitation. Where is now the spirit of Friedrich August Wolf to be found, of whom Franz Passow could say that he seemed a loyal and humanistic spirit with force enough to set half the world aflame? Instead of that a journalistic spirit is arising in the university, often under the name of philosophy; the smooth delivery—the very cosmetics of speech—with Faust and Nathan the Wise for ever on the lips, the accent and the outlook of our worst literary magazines and, more recently, much chatter about our holy German music, and the demand for lectures on Schiller and Goethe,—all this is a sign that the university spirit is beginning to be confused with the Spirit of the Age. Thus the establishment of a higher tribunal, outside the universities, to protect and criticise them with regard to culture, would seem a most valuable thing, and as soon as philosophy can sever itself from the universities and be purified from every unworthy motive or hypocrisy, it will be able to become such a tribunal. It will do its work without state help in money or honours, free from the spirit of the age as well as from any fear of it ; being in fact the judge, as Schopenhauer was, of the so-called culture surrounding it And in this way the philosopher can also be useful to the university, by refusing to be a part of it, but criticising it from afar. Distance will lend dignity.

But, after all, what does the life of a state or the progress of universities matter in comparison with the life of philosophy on earth! For, to say quite frankly what I mean, it is infinitely more important that a philosopher should arise on the earth than that a state or a university should continue. The dignity of philosophy may rise in proportion as the submission to public opinion and the danger to liberty increase; it was at its highest during the convulsions marking the fall of the Roman Republic, and in the time of the Empire, when the names of both philosophy and history became *ingrata principibus nomina*. Brutus shows its dignity better than Plato; his was a time when ethics cease to have commonplaces. Philosophy is not much regarded now, and we may well ask why no great soldier or statesman has taken it up; and the answer is that a thin phantom has met him, under the name of philosophy, the cautious wisdom of the learned professor; and philosophy has soon come to seem ridiculous to him. It ought to have seemed terrible; and men who are called to authority should know the heroic power that has its source there. An American may tell them what a centre of mighty forces a great thinker can prove on this earth. "Beware when the great God lets loose a thinker on this planet," says Emerson. "Then all things are at risk. It is as when a conflagration has broken out in a great city, and no man knows what is safe, or where it will end. There is not a piece of science, but its flank may be turned to-morrow; there is not any literary reputation, not the so-called eternal names of fame, that may not be revised and condemned. . .

. The things which are dear to men at this hour are so on account of the ideas which have emerged on their mental horizon, and which cause the present order of things as a tree bears its apples. A new degree of culture would instantly revolutionise the entire system of human pursuits." If such thinkers are dangerous, it is clear why our university thinkers are not dangerous; for their thoughts bloom as peacefully in the shade of tradition "as ever tree bore its apples." They do not frighten; they carry away no gates of Gaza; and to all their little contemplations one can make the answer of Diogenes when a certain philosopher was praised: "What great result has he to show, who has so long practised philosophy and yet has *hurt* nobody?" Yes, the university philosophy should have on its monument, "It has hurt nobody." But this is rather the praise one gives to an old woman than "to a goddess of truth; and it is not surprising that those who know the goddess only as an old woman are the less men for that, and are naturally neglected by the real men of power.

If this be the case in our time, the dignity of philosophy is trodden in the mire ; and she seems herself to have become ridiculous or insignificant. All her true friends are bound to bear witness against this transformation, at least to show that it is merely her false servants in philosopher's clothing who are so. Or better, they must prove by their own deed that the love of truth has itself awe and power.

Schopenhauer proved this and will continue to prove it, more and more.